THE

CONSTITUTION

&

LAWS

OF

THE REPUBLIC
OF TEXAS

COMPILED BY ROBERT A. IRION,
SECRETARY OF STATE

TO WHICH IS ADDED THE
STATE CONSTITUTION OF 1845

ISBN: 978-0-9829828-3-9

TABLE OF CONTENTS

Publisher's Note

This volume showcases the fruits of the democratic labors of the 1836 Constitutional Convention and the first session of the first congress of the Republic of Texas. It represents the basic principles and ideals that would bind together the inherently independent citizens of this land into a cohesive, sovereign nation under the rule of law.

The original text containing the same was published in 1837 by the *Telegraph* at Houston in a very limited quantity. It is truly a Texana rarity, as are the subsequent volumes of laws passed in the later congresses of the Republic. Unfortunately, the typesetting in the 1837 printing left much to be desired and is somewhat difficult to read. Broken lines and missing letters can be hard on the eyes. And most of the extant copies from which a facsimile might be made have certainly seen better days. For these reasons, we have resisted the temptation to simply create a facsimile of the original work. Doing so would not have accomplished our goal of making these powerful founding documents more accessible to students of Texas history, since a copy of a hard-to-decipher document wouldn't be any easier to read than was the original.

The type has been reset, broken lines restored and missing letters replaced. British-English spelling conventions were favored in the writing of the text and these have been left intact to reflect the educational backgrounds of those who wrote it. What we recognize as American-English spelling conventions today weren't widely introduced and adopted in the United States until 1828. In that year, Noah Webster's *American Dictionary* arrived on the scene, long after the statesmen of the Republic of Texas had received their schooling. Their preferred styles of writing are preserved here in the laws that they enacted.

Michelle M. Haas, Managing Editor
Seven Palms - Rockport, Texas

THE

DECLARATION OF INDEPENDENCE

MADE BY THE

DELEGATES

OF

THE PEOPLE OF TEXAS,

IN

GENERAL CONVENTION, AT WASHINGTON.

On March 2nd, **1836.**

When a government has ceased to protect the lives, liberty and property of the people, from whom its legitimate powers are derived, and for the advancement of whose happiness it was instituted; and so far from being a guarantee for their inestimable and inalienable rights, becomes an instrument in the hands of evil rulers for their oppression. When the federal republican constitution of their country, which they have sworn to support, no longer has a substantial existence, and the whole nature of their government has been forcibly changed, without their consent, from a restricted federative republic, composed of sovereign states, to a consolidated central military despotism, in which every interest is disregarded but that of the army and the priesthood, both the eternal enemies of civil liberty, the ever ready minions of power, and the usual instruments of tyrants. When, long after the spirit of the constitution has departed, moderation is at length so far lost by those in power, that even the semblance of freedom is removed, and the forms themselves of the constitution discontinued, and so far from their petitions and remonstrances being regarded, the agents who bear them are thrown into dungeons, and mercenary armies sent forth to enforce a new government upon them at the point of the bayonet.

When, in consequence of such acts of malfeasance and abduction on the part of the government, anarchy prevails, and civil society is dissolved into its original elements, in such a crisis, the first law of nature, the right of self-preservation, the inherent and inalienable right of the people to appeal to first principles, and take their political affairs into their own hands in extreme cases, enjoins it as a right towards themselves, and a sacred obligation to their posterity, to abolish such government and create another in its stead, calculated to rescue them from impending dangers, and to secure their welfare and happiness.

Nations, as well as individuals, are amenable for their acts to the public opinion of mankind. A statement of a part of our grievances is therefore submitted to an impartial world, in justification of the hazardous but unavoidable step now taken, of severing our political connection with the Mexican people, and assuming an independent attitude among the nations of the earth.

The Mexican government, by its colonization laws, invited and induced the Anglo American population of Texas to colonize its wilderness under the pledged faith of a written constitution, that they should continue to enjoy that constitutional liberty and republican government to which they had been habituated in the land of their birth, the United States of America.

In this expectation they have been cruelly disappointed, inasmuch as the Mexican nation has acquiesced to the late changes made in the government by General Antonio Lopez de Santa Anna, who, having overturned the constitution of his country, now offers, as the cruel alternative, either to abandon our homes, acquired by so many privations, or submit to the most intolerable of all tyranny, the combined despotism of the sword and the priesthood.

It hath sacrificed our welfare to the state of Coahuila, by which our interests have been continually depressed through a jealous and partial course of legislation, carried on at a far distant seat of government, by a hostile majority, in an unknown tongue, and this too, notwithstanding we have petitioned in the humblest terms for the establishment of a separate state government, and have, in accordance with the provisions of the national constitution, presented to the general congress a republican constitution, which was, without a just cause, contemptuously rejected.

It incarcerated in a dungeon, for a long time, one of our citizens, for no other cause but a zealous endeavour to procure the acceptance of our constitution, and the establishment of a state government.

It has failed and refused to secure, on a firm basis, the right of trial by jury, that palladium of civil liberty, and only safe guarantee for the life, liberty, and property of the citizen.

It has failed to establish any public system of education, although possessed of almost boundless resources, (the public domain) and although it is an axiom in political science, that unless a people are educated and enlightened, it is idle to expect the continuance of civil liberty, or the capacity for self government.

It has suffered the military commandants, stationed among us, to exercise arbitrary acts of oppression and tyranny, thus trampling upon the most sacred rights of the citizen, and rendering the military superior to the civil power.

It has dissolved, by force of arms, the state congress of Coahuila and Texas, and obliged our representatives to fly for their lives from the seat of government, thus depriving us of the fundamental political right of representation.

It has demanded the surrender of a number of our citizens, and ordered military detachments to seize and carry them into the interior for trial, in contempt of the civil authorities, and in defiance of the laws and the constitution.

It has made piratical attacks upon our commerce, by commissioning foreign desperadoes, and authorizing them to seize our vessels, and convey the property of our citizens to far distant parts for confiscation.

It denies us the right of worshiping the Almighty according to the dictates of our own conscience, by the support of a national religion, calculated to promote the temporal interest of its human functionaries, rather than the glory of the true and living God.

It has demanded us to deliver up our arms, which are essential to our defence – the rightful property of freemen – and formidable only to tyrannical governments.

It has invaded our country both by sea and by land, with the intent to lay waste our territory, and drive us from our homes; and has now a large mercenary army advancing, to carry on against us a war of extermination.

It has, through its emissaries, incited the merciless savage, with the tomahawk and scalping knife, to massacre the inhabitants of our defenceless frontiers.

It has been, during the whole time of our connection with it, the contemptible sport and victim of successive military revolutions, and hath continually exhibited every characteristic of a weak, corrupt, and tyrannical government.

These, and other grievances, were patiently borne by the people of Texas, until they reached that point at which forbearance ceases to be a virtue. We then took up arms in defence of the national constitution. We appealed to our Mexican brethren for assistance: our appeal has been made in vain; though months have elapsed, no sympathetic response has yet been heard from the interior. We are, therefore, forced to the melancholy conclusion, that the Mexican people have acquiesced in the destruction of their liberty, and the substitution therefor of a military government; that they are unfit to be free, and incapable of self government.

The necessity of self-preservation, therefore, now decrees our eternal political separation.

WE, *therefore, the delegates, with plenary powers, of the people of Texas, in solemn convention assembled, appealing to a candid world for the necessities of our condition, do hereby resolve and declare, that our political connection with the Mexican nation has forever ended, and that the people of Texas do now constitute a* FREE, SOVEREIGN *and* INDEPENDENT REPUBLIC, *and are fully invested with all the rights and attributes which properly belong to independent nations; and, conscious of the rectitude of our intentions, we fearlessly and confidently commit the issue to the supreme Arbiter of the destinies of nations.*

In witness whereof we have hereunto subscribed our names.

RICHARD ELLIS
President and Delegate from Red River,

ALBERT H.S. KIMBALL, *Secretary.*

C. B. Stewart,	John S. Roberts,
James Collinsworth,	Robert Hamilton,
Edwin Waller,	Collin McKinney,
A. Brigham,	A. H. Latimore,
John S. D. Byrom,	James Power,
Francis Ruis,	Sam. Houston,

J. Antonio Navarro,
William D. Lacy,
William Menifee,
John Fisher,
Matthew Caldwell,
William Motley,
Lorenzo de Zavala,
George W. Smyth,
Stephen II. Everett,
Elijah Stepp,
Claiborne West,
William B. Leates,
M. B. Menard,
A. B. Hardin,
John W. Bunton,
Thomas J. Gazley,
R. M. Coleman,
Sterling C. Robertson,
George C. Childress,
Baily Hardiman,
Robert Potter,
Charles Taylor,

Edward Conrad,
Martin Palmer,
James Gaines,
William Clark, jun.,
Sydney O. Pennington,
Samuel P. Carson,
Thomas J. Rusk,
William C. Crawford,
John Turner,
Benjamin Briggs Goodrich,
James G. Swisher,
George W. Barnet,
Jesse Grimes,
E. O. Legrand,
David Thomas,
S. Rhoads Fisher,
John W. Bower,
J. B. Woods,
Andrew Briscoe,
Thomas Barnett.
Jesse B. Badgett,
Stephen W. Blount

I do hereby certify that I have carefully compared the foregoing Declaration, and find it to be a true copy from the original filed in the archives of the Convention.

Given under my hand this 17th day of March, 1836.

Attest,
H. S. KIMBLE,
Secretary of the Convention

CONSTITUTION

OF THE

REPUBLIC OF TEXAS

We, the people of Texas, in order to form a government establish justice, ensure domestic tranquility, provide for the common defence and general welfare; and to secure the blessings of liberty to ourselves, and our posterity, do ordain and establish this constitution.

ARTICLE I.

SECTION 1. The powers of this government shall be divided into three departments, viz: legislative, executive and judicial, which shall remain forever separate and distinct.

SEC. 2. The legislative power shall be vested in a senate and house of representatives, to be styled the congress of the republic of Texas.

SEC. 3. The members of the house of representatives shall be chosen annually, on the first Monday of September each year, until congress shall otherwise provide by law, and shall hold their offices one year from the date of their election.

SEC. 4. No person shall be eligible to a seat in the house of representatives until he shall have attained the age of twenty-five years, shall be a citizen of the republic, and shall have resided in the county or district six months next preceding his election.

SEC. 5. The house of representatives shall not consist of less than twenty-four, nor more than forty members, until the population shall amount to one hundred thousand souls, after which time the whole number of representatives shall not be less than forty, nor more than one hundred: *Provided* however, that each county shall be entitled to at least one representative.

SEC. 6. The house of representatives shall choose their speaker and other officers, and shall have the sole power of impeachment.

SEC. 7. The senators shall be chosen by districts, as nearly equal in free population (free negroes and Indians excepted) as practicable; and the number of senators shall never be less than one third nor more than one half the number of representatives, and each district shall be entitled to one member and no more.

SEC. 8. The senators shall be chosen for the term of three years, on the first Monday in September; shall be citizens of the republic, reside in the district for which they are respectively chosen at least one year before the election; and shall have attained the age of thirty years.

SEC. 9. At the first session of congress after the adoption of this constitution, the senators shall be divided by lot into three classes, as nearly equal as practicable; the seats of the senators of the first class shall be vacated at the end of the first year; of the second class, at the end of the second year; the third class, at the end of the third year, in such a manner that one third shall be chosen each year thereafter.

SEC. 10. The vice president of the republic shall be president of the senate, but shall not vote on any question, unless the senate be equally divided.

SEC. 11. The senate shall choose all other officers of their body, and a president pro tempore, in the absence of the vice president, or whenever he shall exercise the office of president; shall have the sole power to try impeachments, and when sitting as a court of impeachment, shall be under oath; but no conviction shall take place without the concurrence of two thirds of all the members present.

SEC. 12. Judgment in cases of impeachment shall only extend to removal from office, and disqualification to hold any office of honor, trust or profit under this government; but the party shall nevertheless be liable to indictment, trial, judgment and punishment according to law.

SEC. 13. Each house shall be the judge of the elections, qualifications and returns of its own members. Two thirds of each house shall constitute a quorum to do business, but a smaller number may adjourn from day to day, and may compel the attendance of absent members.

SEC. 14. Each house may determine the rules of its own proceedings, punish its members for disorderly behavior, and with the concurrence of two thirds, may expel a member, but not a second time for the same offence.

SEC. 15. Senators and representatives shall receive a compensation for their services, to be fixed by law, but no increase of compensation, or diminution, shall take effect during the session at which such increase or diminution shall have been made. They shall, except in case of treason, felony, or breach of the peace, be privileged from arrest during the session of congress, and in going to and returning from the same; and for any speech or debate in either house they shall not be questioned in any other place.

SEC. 16. Each house may punish, by imprisonment, during the session, any person not a member, who shall be guilty of any disrespect to the house, by any disorderly conduct in their presence.

SEC. 17. Each house shall keep a journal of its proceedings, and publish the same, except such parts as in its judgment require secrecy. When any three members shall desire the yeas and nays on any question, they shall be entered on the journals.

SEC. 18. Neither house, without the consent of the other, shall adjourn for more than three days, nor to any other place than that in which the two houses may be sitting.

SEC. 19. When vacancies happen in either house, the executive shall issue writs of election to fill such vacancies.

SEC. 20. No bill shall become a law until it shall have been read on three several days in each house, and passed by the same, unless, in cases of emergency, two thirds of the members of the house where the bill originated shall deem it expedient to dispense with the rule.

SEC. 21. After a bill shall have been rejected, no bill containing the same substance shall be passed into a law during the same session.

SEC. 22. The style of the laws of the republic shall be, "Be it enacted by the senate and house of representatives of the republic of Texas, in congress assembled."

SEC. 23. No person holding an office of profit under the government shall be eligible to a seat in either house of congress, nor shall any member of either house be eligible to any office which may created, or the profits of which shall be increased during his term of service.

SEC. 24. No holder of public monies or collector thereof, shall be eligible to a seat in either house of congress, until he shall have fully acquitted himself of all responsibility, and shall produce the proper officer's receipt thereof. Members of either house may protest against any act or resolution, and may have such protest entered on the journals of their respective houses.

SEC. 25. No money shall be drawn from the public treasury but in strict accordance with appropriations made by law; and no appropriations shall be made for private or local purposes, unless two thirds of each house concur in such appropriations.

SEC. 26. Every act of congress shall be approved and signed by the president before it becomes a law; but if the president will not approve and sign such act, he shall return it to the house in which it shall have originated, with his reasons for not approving the same, which shall be spread upon the journals of such house, and the bill shall then be reconsidered, and shall not become a law unless it shall then pass by a vote of two thirds of both houses. If any act shall be disapproved by the president, the vote on the reconsideration shall be recorded by ayes and noes. If the president shall fail to return a bill within five days (Sundays excepted) after it shall have been presented for his approval and signature, the same shall become a law, unless the congress prevent its return within the time above specified by adjournment.

SEC. 27. All bills, acts, orders, or resolutions, to which the concurrence of both houses may be necessary, (motions or resolutions for adjournment excepted) shall be approved and signed by the president, or being disapproved, shall be passed by two thirds of both houses, in manner and form as specified in section twenty.

ARTICLE II.

SEC. 1. Congress shall have power to levy and collect taxes and imposts, excise and tonage duties; to borrow money on the faith, credit, and property of the government, to pay the debts and to provide for the common defence and general welfare of the republic.

SEC. 2. To regulate commerce, to coin money, to regulate the value thereof and of foreign coin, to fix the standard of weights and measures, but nothing but gold and silver shall be made a lawful tender.

SEC. 3. To establish post offices and post roads, to grant charters of incorporation, patents and copy rights, and secure to the authors and inventors the exclusive use thereof for a limited time.

SEC. 4. To declare war, grant letters of marque and reprisal, and to regulate captures.

SEC. 5. To provide and maintain an army and navy, and to make all laws and regulations necessary for their government.

SEC. 6. To call out the militia to execute the law, to suppress insurrections, and repel invasion.

SEC. 7. To make all laws which shall be deemed necessary and proper to carry into effect the foregoing express grants of power, and all other powers vested in the government of the republic, or in any officer or department thereof.

ARTICLE III.

SEC. 1. The executive authority of this government shall be vested in a chief magistrate, who shall be styled the president of the republic of Texas.

SEC. 2. The first president elected by the people shall hold his office for the term of two years, and shall be ineligible during the next succeeding term; and all subsequent presidents shall be elected for three years, and be alike ineligible; and in the event of a tie, the house of representatives shall determine between the two highest candidates by a vive voce vote.

SEC. 3. The returns of the elections for president and vice president shall be sealed up and transmitted to the speaker of the house of representatives, by the holders of elections of each county; and the speaker of the house of representatives shall open and publish the returns in presence of a majority of each house of congress.

ARTICLE IV.

SEC. 1. The judicial powers of the government shall be vested in one supreme court, and such inferior courts as the congress may, from time to time, ordain and establish. The judges of the supreme and inferior courts shall hold their offices for four years, be eligible to re-election, and shall, at stated periods, receive for their services a compensation, not to be increased or diminished during the period for which they were elected.

SEC. 2. The republic of Texas shall be divided into convenient judicial districts, not less than three, nor more than eight. There shall be appointed for each district a judge, who shall reside in the same, and hold the courts at such times and places as congress may by law direct.

SEC. 3. In all admiralty and maritime cases, in all cases affecting ambassadors, public ministers or consuls, and in all capital cases, the district courts shall have exclusive original jurisdiction, and original jurisdiction in all civil cases when the matter in controversy amounts to one hundred dollars.

SEC. 4. The judges, by virtue of their offices, shall be conservators of the peace, throughout the republic. The style of all process shall be, "the republic of Texas;" and all prosecutions shall be carried on in the name and by the authority of the same, and conclude, "against the peace and dignity of the republic."

SEC. 5. There shall be a district attorney appointed for each district, whose duties, salaries, perquisites, and term of service shall be fixed by law.

SEC. 6. The clerks of the district courts shall be elected by the qualified voters for members of congress, in the counties where the courts are established, and shall hold their offices for four years, subject to removal by presentment of a grand jury, and conviction of a petit jury.

SEC. 7. The supreme court shall consist of a chief justice and associate judges; the district judges shall compose the associate judges, a majority of whom, with the chief justice, shall constitute a quorum.

SEC. 8. The supreme court shall have appellate jurisdiction only, which shall be conclusive, within the limits of the republic; and shall hold its sessions annually, at such times and places as may be fixed by law: *Provided*, that no judge shall sit in a case in the supreme court tried by him in the court below.

SEC. 9. The judges of the supreme and district courts shall be elected by joint ballot of both houses of congress.

SEC. 10. There shall be in each county a county court, and such justices' courts as the congress may, from time to time, establish.

SEC. 11. The republic shall be divided into convenient counties, but no new county shall be established, unless it be done on the petition of one hundred free male inhabitants of the territory sought to be laid off and established; and unless the said territory shall contain nine hundred square miles.

SEC. 12. There shall be appointed for each county, a convenient number of justices of the peace, one sheriff, one coroner, and a sufficient number of constables, who shall hold their offices for two years, to be elected by the qualified voters of the district or county, as congress may direct. Justices of the peace and sheriffs shall be commissioned by the president.

SEC. 13. The congress shall, as early as practicable, introduce, by statute, the common law of England, with such modifications as our circumstances, in their judgment, may require; and in all criminal cases, the common law shall be the rule of decision.

ARTICLE V.

SEC. 1. Ministers of the gospel being, by their profession, dedicated to God and the care of souls, ought not to be diverted from the great duties of their functions: therefore, no minister of the gospel, or priest of any denomination whatever, shall be eligible to the office of the executive of the republic, nor to a seat in either branch of the congress of the same.

SEC. 2. Each member of the senate and house of representatives shall, before they proceed to business, take an oath to support the constitution, as follows;

"I, A. B., do solemnly swear [or affirm, as the case may be] that, as a member of this general congress, I will support the constitution of the republic, and that I will not propose or assent to any bill, vote, or resolution, which shall appear to me injurious to the people."

SEC. 3. Every person who shall be chosen or appointed to any office of trust or profit shall, before entering on the duties thereof, take an oath to support the constitution of the republic, and also an oath of office.

ARTICLE VI.

SEC. 1. No person shall be eligible to the office of president who shall not have attained the age of thirty-five years, shall be a citizen of the republic at the time of the adoption of this constitution, or an inhabitant of this republic at least three years immediately preceding his election.

SEC. 2. The president shall enter on the duties of his office on the second Monday in December next succeeding his election, and shall remain in office until his successor shall be duly qualified.

SEC. 3. The president shall, at stated times, receive a compensation for his services, which shall not be increased or diminished during his continuance in office; and before entering upon the duties of his office, he shall take and subscribe the following oath or affirmation:

"I, A. B., president of the republic of Texas, do solemnly and sincerely swear (or affirm, as the case may be) that I will faithfully execute the duties of my office, and to the best of my abilities preserve, protect, and defend the constitution of the Republic."

SEC. 4. He shall be commander-in-chief of the army and navy of the republic, and militia thereof, but he shall not command in person without the authority of a resolution of congress. He shall have power to remit fines and forfeitures, and to grant reprieves and pardons, except in cases of impeachment.

SEC. 5. He shall, with the advice and consent of two-thirds of the senate, make treaties; and with the consent of the senate, appoint ministers and consuls, and all officers whose offices are established by this constitution, not herein otherwise provided for.

SEC. 6. The president shall have power to fill all vacancies that may happen during the recess of the senate; but he shall report the same to the senate within ten days after the next congress shall convene; and should the senate reject the same, the president shall not re-nominate the same individual to the same office.

SEC. 7. He shall, from time to time, give congress information of the state of the republic, and recommend for their consideration such measures as he may deem necessary. He may, upon extraordinary occasions, convene both houses, or either of them. In the event of a disagreement as to the time of adjournment, he may adjourn them to such time as he may think proper. He shall receive all foreign ministers. He shall see that the laws be faithfully executed, and shall commission all the officers of the republic.

SEC. 8. There shall be a seal of the republic, which shall be kept by the president, and used by him officially; it shall be called the great seal of the republic of Texas.

SEC. 9. All grants and commissions shall be in the name, and by the authority of the republic of Texas, shall be sealed with the great seal, and signed by the president.

SEC. 10. The president shall have power, by and with the advice and consent of the senate, to appoint a secretary of state and such other heads of executive departments as may be established by law, who shall remain in office during the term of service of the president, unless sooner removed by the president, with the advice and consent of the senate.

SEC. 11. Every citizen of the republic who has attained the age of twenty-one years, and shall have resided six months within the district or county where the election is held, shall be entitled to vote for members of the general congress.

SEC. 12. All elections shall be by ballot, unless congress shall otherwise direct.

SEC. 13. All elections by joint vote of both houses of congress shall be viva voce, shall be entered on the journals, and a majority of the votes shall be necessary to a choice.

SEC. 14. A vice president shall be chosen at every election for president, in the same manner, continue in office for the same time, and shall possess the same qualifications of the president. In voting for president and vice president, the electors shall distinguish for whom they vote as president, and for whom as vice president.

SEC. 15. In cases of impeachment, removal from office, death, resignation, or absence of the president from the republic, the vice president shall exercise the powers and discharge the duties of the president until a successor be duly qualified, or until the president, who may be absent or impeached, shall return or be acquitted.

SEC. 16. The president, vice president, and all civil officers of the republic, shall be removable from office by impeachment for, and on conviction of, treason, bribery, and other high crimes and misdemeanors.

SCHEDULE.

SEC. 1. That no inconvenience may arise from the adoption of this constitution, it is declared by this convention that all laws now in force in Texas, and not inconsistent with this constitution, shall remain in full force until declared void, repealed, altered, or expire by their own limitation.

SEC. 2. All fines, penalties, forfeitures and escheats, which have accrued to Coahuila and Texas, or Texas, shall accrue to this republic.

SEC. 3. Every male citizen, who is, by this constitution, a citizen, and shall be otherwise qualified, shall be entitled to hold any office or place of honor, trust, or profit under the republic, any thing in this constitution to the contrary notwithstanding.

SEC. 4. The first president and vice president that shall be appointed after the adoption of this constitution, shall be chosen by this convention, and shall immediately enter on the duties of their offices, and shall hold said offices until their successors be elected and qualified, as prescribed in this constitution, and shall have the same qualifications, be invested with the same powers, and perform the same duties which are required and conferred on the executive head of the republic by this constitution.

SEC. 5. The president shall issue writs of election directed to the officers authorized to hold elections of the several counties, requiring them to cause an election to be held for president, vice president, representatives, and senators to congress, at the time and mode prescribed by this constitution, which election shall be conducted in the manner that elections have been heretofore conducted. The president, vice president, and members of congress, when duly elected, shall continue to discharge the duties of their respective offices for the time and manner prescribed by this constitution, until their successors be duly qualified.

SEC. 6. Until the first enumeration shall be made, as directed by this constitution, the precinct of Austin shall be entitled to one representative; the precinct of Brazoria to two representatives; the precinct of Bexar two representatives; the precinct of Colorado one representative; Sabine one; Gonzales one; Goliad one; Harrisburg one; Jasper one; Jefferson one; Liberty one; Matagorda one; Mina two; Nacogdoches two; Red River three; Victoria one; San Augustine two; Shelby two; Refugio one; San Patricio one; Washington two; Milam one; and Jackson one representative.

SEC. 7. Until the first enumeration shall be made, as described by this constitution, the senatorial districts shall be composed of the following precincts: Bexar shall be entitled to one senator; San Patricio, Refugio and Goliad one; Brazoria one; Mina and Gonzales one; Nacogdoches one; Red River one; Shelby and Sabine one; Washington one; Matagorda, Jackson and Victoria one; Austin and Colorado one; San Augustine one; Milam one; Jasper and Jefferson one; and Liberty and Harrisburg one senator.

SEC. 8. All judges, sheriffs, commissioners, and other civil officers shall remain in office, and in the discharge of the powers and duties of their respective offices, until there shall be others appointed or elected under the constitution.

GENERAL PROVISIONS.

SEC. 1. Laws shall be made to exclude from office, from the right of suffrage, and from serving on juries, those who shall hereafter be convicted of bribery, perjury, or other high crimes and misdemeanors.

SEC. 2. Returns of all elections for officers who are to be commissioned by the president, shall be made to the secretary of state of this republic.

SEC. 3. The presidents and heads of departments shall keep their offices at the seat of government, unless removed by the permission of congress, or unless in cases of emergency in time of war, the public interest may require their removal.

SEC. 4. The president shall make use of his private seal until a seal of the republic shall be provided.

SEC. 5. It shall be the duty of congress, as soon as circumstances will permit, to provide by law, a general system of education.

SEC. 6. All free white persons who shall emigrate to this republic, and who shall, after a residence of six months, make oath before some competent authority that he intends to reside permanently in the same, and shall swear to support this constitution, and that he will bear true allegiance to the republic of Texas, shall be entitled to all the privileges of citizenship.

SEC. 7. So soon as convenience will permit, there shall be a penal code formed on principles of reformation, and not of vindictive justice; and the civil and criminal laws shall be revised, digested, and arranged under different heads; and all laws relating to land titles shall be translated, revised and promulgated.

SEC. 8. All persons who shall leave the country for the purpose of evading a participation in the present struggle, or shall refuse to participate in it, or shall give aid or assistance to the present enemy, shall forfeit all rights of citizenship, and such lands as they may hold in the republic.

SEC. 9. All persons of color who were slaves for life previous to their emigration to Texas, and who are now held in bondage, shall remain in the like state of servitude: *provided*, the said slave shall be the bona fide property of the person so holding said slave as aforesaid. Congress shall pass no laws to prohibit emigrants from bringing their slaves into the republic with them, and holding them by the same tenure by which such slaves were held in the United States; nor shall congress have power to emancipate slaves; nor shall any slave holder be allowed to emancipate his or her slave or slaves without the consent of congress, unless he or she shall send his or her slave or slaves without the limits of the republic. No free person of African descent, either in whole or in part, shall be permitted to reside permanently in the republic, without the consent of congress; and the importation or admission of Africans or negroes into this republic, excepting from the United States of America, is forever prohibited, and declared to be piracy.

SEC. 10. All persons (Africans, the descendants of Africans, and Indians excepted) who were residing in Texas on the day of the declaration of independence, shall be considered citizens of the republic, and entitled to all the privileges of such. All citizens now living in Texas, who have not received their portion of land, in like manner as colonists, shall be entitled to their land in the following proportion and manner: Every head of a family shall be entitled to one league and labor of land; and every single man of the age of seventeen and upwards, shall be entitled to the third part of one league of land. All citizens who may have previously to the adoption of this constitution, received their league of land as heads of families, and their quarter of a league of land as single persons, shall receive such additional quantity as will make the quantity of land received by them equal to one league and labor, and one third of a league, unless by bargain, sale, or exchange, they have transferred or may henceforth transfer their right to said land, or a portion thereof, to some other citizen of the republic: and in such case, the person to whom such right shall have been transferred shall be entitled to the same, as fully and amply as the person making the transfer might or could have been. — No alien shall hold land in Texas, except by titles emanating directly from the government of this republic. But if any citizen of this republic should die intestate or otherwise, his children or heirs shall inherit his estate, and aliens shall have a reasonable time to take possession of and dispose of the same, in a manner hereafter to be pointed out by law. Orphan children whose parents were entitled to land under the colonization laws of Mexico, and who now reside in the republic, shall be entitled to all the rights which their parents were possessed at the time of their death. The citizens of the republic shall not be compelled to reside on the land, but shall have their lines plainly marked.

All orders of survey legally obtained by any citizen of the republic, from any legally authorized commissioner, prior to the act of the late consultation closing the land offices, shall be valid. In all cases the actual settler and occupant of the soil shall be entitled, in locating his land, to include his improvement, in preference to all other claims not acquired previous to his settlement, according to the law of the land and this constitution — *provided*, that nothing herein contained shall prejudice the rights of any other citizen from whom a settler may hold land by rent or lease.

And whereas, the protection of the public domain from unjust and fraudulent claims, and quieting the people in the enjoyment of their lands, is one of the great duties of this convention; and whereas the legislature of Coahuila and Texas having passed an act in the year 1834, in behalf of General John T. Mason of New York, and another on the 14th day of March, 1835, under which the enormous amount of eleven hundred leagues of land has been claimed by sundry individuals, some of whom reside in foreign countries, and are not citizens of the republic — which said acts are contrary to articles fourth, twelfth, and fifteenth of the laws of 1824 of the general congress of Mexico, and one of said acts, for that cause has, by said general congress of Mexico, been declared null and void: It is hereby declared that the said act of 1834, in favor of John T. Mason, and of the 14th of March, 1835, of the said legislature of Coahuila and Texas, and each and every grant founded thereon, is, and was from the beginning, null and void; and all surveys made under pretence of authority derived from said acts, are hereby declared to be nail and void: and all eleven league claims, located within twenty leagues of the boundary line between Texas and the United States of America, which have been located contrary to the laws of Mexico, are hereby declared to be null and void. And whereas many surveys and titles to lands have been made whilst most of the people of Texas were absent from home, serving in the campaign against Bexar, it is hereby declared that all the surveys and locations of land made since the act of the late consultation closing the land offices, and all titles to land made since that time, are, and shall be null and void.

And whereas the present unsettled state of the country and the general welfare of the people demand that the operations of the land office, and the whole land system shall be suspended until persons serving in the army can have a fair and equal chance with those remaining at home, to select and locate their lands, it is hereby declared, that no survey or title which may hereafter be made shall be valid, unless such survey or title shall be authorized by this convention, or some future congress of the republic. And with a view to the simplification of the land system, and the protection of the people and the government from litigation and fraud, a general land office shall be established, where all the land titles of the republic shall be registered, and the whole territory of the republic shall be sectionized, in a manner hereafter to be prescribed by law, which shall enable the officers of the government or any citizen, to ascertain with certainty the lands that are vacant, and those lands which may he covered with valid titles.

SEC. 11. Any amendment or amendments to this constitution, may be proposed in the house of representatives or senate, and if the same shall be agreed to by a majority of the members elected to each of the two houses, such proposed amendment or amendments shall be entered on the journals, with the yeas and nays thereon, and referred to the congress then next to be chosen, and shall be published for three months previous to the election; and if the congress next chosen as aforesaid, shall pass said amendment or amendments by a vote of two-thirds of all the members elected to each house, then it shall be the duty of said congress to submit said proposed amendment or amendments to the people, in such manner and at such times as the congress shall prescribe; and if the people shall approve and ratify such amendment or amendments by a majority of the electors qualified to vote for members of congress voting thereon, such amendment or amendments shall become a part of this constitution: *Provided*, however, that no amendment or amendments be referred to the people oftener than once in three years.

DECLARATION OF RIGHTS.

This declaration of rights is declared to be a part of this constitution, and shall never be violated on any pretence whatever. And in order to guard against the transgression of the high powers which we have delegated, we declare that every thing in this bill of rights contained, and every other right not hereby delegated, is reserved to the people.

First. All men, when they form a social compact, have equal rights, and no men or set of men are entitled to exclusive public privileges or emoluments from the community.

Second. All political power is inherent in the people, and all free governments are founded on their authority, and instituted for their benefit; and they have at all times an inalienable right to alter their government in such manner as they may think proper.

Third. No preference shall be given by law to any religious denomination or mode of worship over another, but every person shall be permitted to worship God according to the dictates of his own conscience.

Fourth. Every citizen shall be at liberty to speak, write, or publish his opinions on any subject, being responsible for the abuse of that privilege. No law shall ever be passed to curtail the liberty of speech or of the press; and in all prosecutions for libels, the truth may be given in evidence, and the jury shall have the right to determine the law and fact, under the direction of the court.

Fifth. The people shall be secure in their persons, houses, papers, and possessions, from all unreasonable searches and seizures, and no warrant shall issue to search any place or seize any person or thing, without describing the place to be searched or the person or thing to be seized, without probable cause, supported by oath or affirmation.

Sixth. In all criminal prosecutions the accused shall have the right of being heard, by himself, or counsel, or both; he shall have the right to demand the nature and cause of the accusation, shall be confronted with the witnesses against him, and have compulsory process for obtaining witnesses in his favor. And in all prosecutions by presentment or indictment, he shall have the right to a speedy and public trial, by an impartial jury; he shall not be compelled to give evidence against himself, or be deprived of life, liberty, or property, but by due course of law. And no freeman shall be holden to answer for any criminal charge, but on presentment or indictment by a grand jury, except in the land and naval forces, or in the militia when in actual service in time of war or public danger, or in cases of impeachment.

Seventh. No citizen shall be deprived of privileges, outlawed, exiled, or in any manner disfranchised, except by due course of the law of the land.

Eighth. No title of nobility, hereditary privileges or honors, shall ever be granted or conferred in this republic. No person holding any office of profit or trust shall, without the consent of congress, receive from any foreign state any present, office, or emolument of any kind.

Ninth. No person, for the same offence, shall be twice put in jeopardy of life or limbs. And the right of trial by jury shall remain inviolate.

Tenth. All persons shall be bailable by sufficient security, unless for capital crimes, when the proof is evident or presumption strong; and the privilege of the writ of "habeas corpus" shall not be suspended, except in case of rebellion or invasion the public safety may require it.

Eleventh. Excessive bail shall not be required, nor excessive fine imposed, or cruel or unusual punishments inflicted. All courts shall be open, and every man for any injury done him in his lands, goods, person, or reputation, shall have remedy by due course of law.

Twelfth. No person shall be imprisoned for debt in consequence of inability to pay.

CONSTITUTION

Thirteenth. No person's particular services shall be demanded, nor property taken or applied to public use, unless by the consent of himself or his representative, without just compensation being made therefor according to law.

Fourteenth. Every citizen shall have the right to bear arms in defence of himself and the republic. The military shall at all times and in all cases be subordinate to the civil power.

Fifteenth. The sure and certain defence of a free people is a well regulated militia; and it shall be the duty of the legislature to enact such laws as may be necessary to the organizing of the militia of this republic.

Sixteenth. Treason against this republic shall consist only in levying war against it, or adhering to its enemies, giving them aid and support. No retrospective or ex-post facto law, or laws impairing the obligation of contracts, shall be made.

Seventeenth. Perpetuities or monopolies are contrary to the genius of a free government, and shall not be allowed; nor shall the law of primogeniture or entailments ever be in force in this republic.

The foregoing constitution was unanimously adopted by the delegates of Texas, in convention assembled, at the town of Washington, on the seventeenth day of March, in the year of our Lord one thousand eight hundred and thirty-six, and of the Independence of the Republic, the first year.

In witness whereof, we have hereunto subscribed our names.

RICHARD ELLIS,
President and Delegate from Red River.

ALBERT H. S. KIMBLE, *Secretary*

C. B. Stewart,	John S. Roberts,
James Collinsworth,	Robert Hamilton,
Edwin Waller,	Collin McKinney,
A. Brigham,	A. H. Latimore,
John S. D. Byrom,	James Power,
Francis Ruis,	Sam. Houston,
J. Antonio Navarro,	Edward Conrad,
William D. Lacy,	Martin Palmer,
William Menifee,	James Gaines,
John Fisher,	William Clark, jun.,
Matthew Caldwell,	Sydney O. Pennington,

William Motley,
Lorenzo de Zavala,
George W. Smyth,
Stephen H. Everett,
Elijah Stepp,
Claiborne West,
William B. Leates,
M. B. Menard,
A. B. Hardin,
John W. Bunton,
Thomas J. Gazley,
R. M. Coleman,
Sterling C. Robertson,
George C. Children,
Baily Hardiman,
Robert Potter,
Charles Taylor,

Samuel P. Carson,
Thomas J. Rusk,
William C. Crawford,
John Turner,
Benjamin Briggs Goodrich,
James G. Swisher,
George W. Barnet,
Jesse Grimes,
E. O. Legrand,
David Thomas,
S. Rhoads Fisher,
John W. Bower,
J. B, Woods,
Andrew Briscoe,
Thomas Barnett,
Jesse B. Badgett,
Stephen W. Blount

I do hereby certify that I have carefully compared the foregoing Constitution, and find it to be a true copy from the original filed in the archives of the Convention.

Given under my hand this 17th day of March, 1836.

Attest,

H. S. KIMBLE,
Secretary of the Convention

LAWS

OF THE

REPUBLIC OF TEXAS

AN ACT

Authorizing the President of the Republic to appoint his cabinet officers.

Be it enacted by the senate and house of representatives of the republic of Texas, in congress assembled, That the president be and he is hereby authorized to appoint, by and with the advice and consent of the senate, in addition to the secretary of state, a secretary each of the treasury, war, and navy departments; also, an attorney general; which officers, when so appointed shall constitute the president's cabinet.

SEC. 2. *Be it further enacted,* That the president be, and he is hereby authorized to fill any vacancies in said offices, which may occur during the recess of the senate, either by death or resignation.

IRA INGRAM,
Speaker of the house of representatives.

MIRABEAU B. LAMAR,
President of the senate.

Approved Oct. 25, 1836.

SAM. HOUSTON.

JOINT RESOLUTION

Recognizing the orders of General T. J. Rusk, relative to certain mail routes and carriers.

Resolved by the senate and house of representatives of the republic of Texas, in congress assembled, That the orders of General T. J. Rusk, establishing certain mail routes, and employing carriers, be recognised; and that the paymaster be instructed to audit the accounts.

IRA INGRAM,
Speaker of the house of representatives.
RICHARD ELLIS,
President pro. tem. of the senate.
Approved Nov. 3, 1836.

SAM. HOUSTON.

JOINT RESOLUTION

Confirming the Contract of Major General Memican Hunt.

Be it resolved by the senate and house of representatives of the republic of Texas, in congress assembled, That the contract entered into by the government *ad interim* with Memican Hunt, on the 11th of June last, be, and the same is hereby recognised and re-confirmed by the existing government of this republic; and that the president be authorized and instructed forthwith to inform said Hunt of the same.

IRA INGRAM,
Speaker of the house of representatives.
MIRABEAU B. LAMAR,
President of the senate.
Approved Nov. 7, 1836.

SAM. HOUSTON.

AN ACT

For the relief of Erastus Smith.

Whereas, it is both just and wise in a government to reward bravery, gallant daring, and exalted patriotism in her citizens; and whereas Erastus Smith, usually known and called *"Deaf Smith,"* unites these qualities in an exalted degree, together with his heavy losses, constant services, and self sacrifices in the cause of Texas and liberty; therefore,

LAWS

SEC. 1. *Be it enacted by the senate and house of representatives of the republic of Texas, in congress assembled*, That there shall be and is hereby granted to Erastus Smith, his heirs or assigns forever, any house and lot in the city of Bexar, which may be confiscated to the public use, under the provisions and by authority of any law or laws of this republic

SEC. 2. *And be it further enacted*, That it shall be lawful for said Erastus Smith, his heirs or assigns, to avail himself of the benefit of this act at as early a period as he may desire, from and after said confiscated property shall be lawfully ascertained.

SEC. 3. *And be it further enacted*, That in further consideration of what is justly due to said Erastus Smith, his heirs or assigns forever, he shall be, and is hereby granted one league and one labor of public land, to be by him, his heirs or assigns, selected of any of the public domain of Texas, so soon as the land offices are opened for entry and location: *provided* that no public property, such as forts, court houses, calibooses, churches, public squares, &c. shall be granted to said Erastus Smith.

IRA INGRAM,
Speaker of the house of representatives.
MIRABEAU B. LAMAR,
President of the senate.

Approved Nov. 11, 1836.

SAM. HOUSTON.

———

JOINT RESOLUTION

For sending a Minister to the United States of America.

Whereas, the good people of Texas, in accordance with a proclamation of his Excellency D. G. Burnet, president *ad interim* of the republic, did, on the first Monday of September last past, at an election held for president, vice president, senators, and representatives of congress, vote to be annexed to the United States of America, with an unanimity unparalleled in the annals of the elective franchise, only ninety-three of the whole population voting against it:

Be it therefore resolved by the senate and house of representatives of the republic of Texas, in congress assembled, That the president be, and he is hereby authorized and requested to despatch forthwith to the government of the United States of America, a minister, vested with ample and plenary powers to enter into negotiations and treaties with the United States government for the recognition of the independence of Texas, and for an immediate annexation to the United States; a measure required by the almost unanimous voice of the people of Texas, and fully concurred in by the present congress.

IRA INGRAM,
Speaker of the house of representatives.
MIRABEAU B. LAMAR,
President of the senate.
Approved Nov. 16, 1836.
SAM. HOUSTON.

————

AN ACT

Providing for an increase of the Navy.

SEC. 1. *Be it enacted by the senate and home of representatives of the republic of Texas, in congress assembled*, That the present naval force of that Republic shall be, as soon as practicable, increased by the building or purchase of the following number and description of vessels, viz: One sloop of war, mounting twenty-four guns, and of such a draft of water as will enable her to enter the port of Galveston; also two armed steam vessels, drawing, when loaded, not exceeding six feet water, built upon the most approved plan, and capable of transporting seven hundred and fifty men and provisions each: and two schooners mounting eleven guns each, carrying two topsails, and not to draw over eight feet and a half water.

SEC. 2. *And be it further enacted*, That the president shall forthwith, by and with the consent of the senate, appoint some proper person, or persons, whose duty it shall be to proceed immediately to the United States of America, and purchase or contract for and superintend the building of the above named number and description of vessels.

IRA INGRAM,
Speaker of the house of representatives.
MIRABEAU B. LAMAR,
President of the senate.

Approved Nov. 18, 1836.

SAM. HOUSTON.

AN ACT

Providing rations, and other comforts, for soldiers, and widows of soldiers, at the town of Columbia.

SEC. 1. *Be it enacted by the senate and house of representatives of the republic of Texas, in congress assembled*, That the president of the republic of Texas shall be, and he is hereby authorised and empowered to appoint one quarter master, and such number of commissaries as he may deem requisite to discharge the duties herein prescribed.

SEC. 2. *And be it further enacted*, That the quarter master shall provide tents and rations for all soldiers that may be here at the town of Columbia, and detained on business with the government; it shall also be his duty to provide for the sick, and also for widows and their families.

SEC. 3. *And be it further enacted*, That the president be, and is hereby further authorised and empowered to order the quarter master to make use of any or all the public cattle, recently driven to this place for the purposes specified in the second section of this act.

SEC. 4. *And be it further enacted*, That it shall be the duty of the quarter master to make out a clear, concise, and full report of all disbursements and expenditures, the names of each and every individual, the length of time that they have been furnished, and the amount furnished to each one, at least once in every month.

SEC. 5. *And be it further enacted*, That the president of the Republic shall be, and is hereby fully authorised and empowered, to cause to be defrayed by this government, all expenses that may be incurred under the provisions of the foregoing act.

IRA INGRAM,

Speaker of the house of representatives.

MIRABEAU B. LAMAR,

President of the senate.

Approved Nov. 18, 1836.

SAM. HOUSTON.

———

AN ACT

To authorise the President to negotiate a loan on the bonds of the government not exceeding five millions of dollars.

SEC. 1. *Be it enacted by the senate and house of representatives of the republic of Texas, in congress assembled,* That the president of this republic be, and he is hereby fully authorised to issue bonds of this republic, for the sum of one thousand dollars each, not exceeding five millions of dollars; which bonds shall be signed by the president and secretary of state, and countersigned by the secretary of the treasury; shall be negotiable by simple endorsement, and shall bear an interest on the face thereof, at a rate not exceeding ten per cent, per annum, to be paid to the holders thereof at such times and place as may be stipulated in said bonds. Said bonds to be prepared as soon as practicable under the direction of the president, and made redeemable in thirty years from the day of date.

SEC. 2. *Be it further enacted,* That the president, by and with the advice and consent of the senate, shall appoint two commissioners into whose hands said bonds shall be delivered by the president, who shall immediately proceed to the United States of America, for the purpose of negotiating said bonds; but if said commissioners should not be able to negotiate the sale of said bonds in the United States of America, then, in that case, they are authorised and hereby required to proceed to Europe for the purpose of effecting said negotiations.

SEC. 3. *Be it further enacted*, That in case of the death or resignation of said commissioners, or either of them during the recess of congress, the president is hereby fully empowered to fill such vacancy, or vacancies, until the meeting of the next congress.

SEC. 4. *Be it further enacted*, That said commissioners are hereby required to correspond with the secretary of the treasury of this republic, informing him of the progress of their negotiations; and that said commissioners be, and are hereby required to pay over to said secretary of the treasury all monies which they may receive from the sale of said bonds, or any portion thereof.

SEC. 5. *Be it further enacted*, That it shall be the duty of the secretary of the treasury to lay before each and every congress, early in every session, a full statement of all such sale or sales of said bonds, as may have been effected, showing the terms and conditions of said sale or sales, the expenses accruing thereon, and what dispositions hare been made of the proceeds of the same.

SEC. 6. *Be it further enacted*, That said commissioners are hereby authorised to negotiate two millions of dollars of said bonds redeemable in a less time than thirty, but not for a shorter period than five years.

SEC. 7. *Be it further enacted*, That if any bank or banks shall become the purchaser, or purchasers, of any portion of said bonds, then and in that case, said commissioners are hereby authorised to stipulate that the notes of said bank or banks shall be received at par, in payment of all public dues of this republic, to the amount of their loan or purchase of said bonds, so long as said bank or banks continue solvent and specie paying; and if any bank or banks become the purchaser or purchasers of any portion of said bonds, the said commissioners shall specify on the face of said bond or bonds, that they are redeemable and payable in the notes of said bank or banks.

SEC. 8. *Be it further enacted*, That if any bank or banks which may purchase said bond or bonds, or any portion of them shall fail, stop payment, or refuse to redeem its or their notes with specie, then and in that case the government of Texas shall have the privilege of terminating the loan with said bank at any time, by a payment of the principal and interest of the same.

SEC. 9. *Be it further enacted*, That said commissioners are hereby authorised to give to the purchasers of said bonds the privilege of at any time taking the amount of their loans or purchases in land, at the minimum government price; or if the public lands are sold at auction, that said lenders or purchasers shall be allowed to bid, and pay the amount of their bids with any of such bonds as they may have purchased.

SEC. 10. *And be it further enacted,* That for the punctual payment of the interest, and final redemption of said bonds, the public faith is hereby solemnly pledged; and also all the proceeds of the sales of the public domain; and also all the taxes on lands which may accrue to this government after the year 1838, are hereby reserved and appropriated for that special purpose.

IRA INGRAM,
Speaker of the house of representatives.
MIRABEAU B. LAMAR,
President of the senate.
Approved Nov. 18, 1836.
SAM. HOUSTON.

———

JOINT RESOLUTION

Explaining the different acts in relation to the service of Volunteers, and extending the acts relating to bounty lands.

SEC. 1. *Be it resolved by the senate and house of representatives of the republic of Texas, in congress assembled,* That the pay of volunteers from the United States and elsewhere shall commence from the time of their embodying and leaving home, provided said time shall not exceed sixty days prior to their being mustered into service of the republic of Texas, at which time their term of service will commence.

SEC. 2. *Be it further resolved,* That the provisions of the ordinances granting the lands to volunteers from the United States and elsewhere, be so construed as to extend to all who have rendered service as volunteers in the army of the republic of Texas.

SEC. 3. *And be it further resolved,* That all volunteers who have entered the service of the republic of Texas since the first day of July last, shall be entitled to the same pay and bounties of land as those who entered the service prior to that time.

IRA INGRAM,
Speaker of the house of representatives.

MIRABEAU B. LAMAR,
President of the senate.

Vetoed by the president, and passed by a constitutional majority of the house of representatives, November 23, 1836.

IRA INGRAM,
Speaker of the house of representatives.

This act was vetoed by the president, and passed by a constitutional majority of the senate, November 24,1836.

RICHARD ELLIS,
President pro tem. of the senate.

———

AN ACT

For establishing Rules and Articles for the government of the Armies of the Republic of Texas.

Be it enacted by the senate and house of representatives of the republic of Texas, in congress assembled, That from and after the passing of this act, the following shall be the rules and regulations by which the armies of said republic of Texas shall be governed.

ART. 1. Any officer or soldier, who shall use contemptuous or disrespectful language towards the president of the republic, against the vice president or congress thereof, if a commissioned officer, shall be cashiered or otherwise punished, as a court martial shall direct; if a non-commissioned officer, or soldier, he shall suffer such punishment as shall be inflicted on him by the sentence of a court martial.

ART. 2. Any officer or soldier, who shall behave himself with contempt or disrespect towards his commanding officer, shall be punished, according to the nature of his offence, by the judgment of a court martial.

ART. 3. Any officer or soldier, who shall begin, cause, excite, or join in any meeting or sedition in any troop or company, in the service of the republic, or in any party, post, detachment, or guard, shall suffer death, or such punishment as by a court martial shall be inflicted.

ART. 4. Any officer, non-commissioned officer, or soldier, who, being present at any mutiny, or sedition, and does not use his utmost endeavours to suppress the same, or coming to the knowledge of any intended mutiny, does not, without delay, give information thereof to his commanding officer, shall be punished by the sentence of a court martial with death, or otherwise, according to the nature of his offence.

ART. 5. Any officer, or soldier, who shall strike his superior officer, or lift any weapon, or offer any violence against him, being in the execution of his office, on any pretence what ever, or shall disobey any lawful command of his superior officer, shall suffer death, or such other punishment as shall, according to the nature of his offence, be inflicted upon him by the sentence of a court martial.

ART. 6. Every non-commissioned officer, or soldier, who shall enlist himself in the regular service of this republic, shall, at the time of his enlisting, or within six days afterwards, have the articles for the government of the armies of the republic read to him, and shall, by the officer who enlisted him, or by the commanding officer of the troop or company in which he was enlisted, be taken before the next civil or chief magistrate of any city or town corporate, not being an officer of the army; or where recourse cannot be had to the civil magistrate, before the judge advocate; and in his presence shall take the following oath or affirmation:

"I,   do solemnly swear or affirm, (as the case may be,) that I will bear true allegiance to the republic of Texas, and that I will serve her honestly and faithfully against all her enemies, or opposers whatsoever, and observe and obey the orders of the president of the republic, and the officers appointed over me, according to the rules and articles for the government of the armies of the republic."

Which justice, magistrate, or judge advocate, is to give the officer a certificate, stating that the man enlisted did take the oath or affirmation.

LAWS

ART. 7. After a non-commissioned officer or soldier shall have been duly enlisted and sworn, he shall not be dismissed the service without a discharge in writing; and no discharge granted to him shall be sufficient which is not signed by the field officer of the regiment to which he belongs; or commanding officer, when no field officer of the regiment is present; and no discharge shall be given to a non-commissioned officer, or soldier, before his term of service shall have expired, but by order of the president, the secretary of war, the commanding officer of a department, or the sentence of a general court martial; nor shall a commissioned officer be discharged but by order of the president of the republic, or by order of a general court martial.

ART. 8. Every colonel or officer commanding a regiment, troop, or company, and actually quartered with it, may give furloughs to non-commissioned officers and soldiers in such numbers, and for such a length of time, as he shall judge to be most consistent with the good of the service; and a captain or other inferior officer, commanding a troop or company, or in any garrison, fort, or barrack of the republic, (his field officer being absent) may give furloughs to non-commissioned officers or soldiers, for a term not exceeding twenty days in six months; but not to more than two persons to be absent at the same time, excepting; some extraordinary occasion should require it.

ART. 9. At every muster the commanding officer of each regiment, troop, or company, there present, shall give to the inspector general, or other officer, who musters said regiment, troop, or company, certificates, signed by himself, signifying how long such officers as shall not appear at said muster have been absent, and the reason of their absence. In like manner every commanding officer of every troop or company, shall give certificates, signifying the reasons of the absence of the non-commissioned officers, and private soldiers, which reasons and time of absence shall be inserted in the muster rolls, opposite the respective names of the absent officers and soldiers. The certificates shall, together with the muster rolls, he transmitted by the inspector general, or other officer mustering, to the secretary of war, as speedily as the distance of the place will admit.

ART. 10. Every officer, who shall be convicted before a general court martial, of having signed a false certificate, relating to the absence of either officer or private soldier, or relative to his or their pay, shall be cashiered.

ART. 11. Every officer who shall make, knowingly, a false muster roll of man or horse, and every officer or inspector general who shall willingly sign, direct, or allow the signing of muster rolls, wherein such false muster is contained, shall, upon proof made by two witnesses, before a general court martial, be cashiered; and shall be thereby utterly disabled to have or hold any office or employment in the service of the republic.

ART. 12. Any officer who shall presume to muster a person as a soldier, who is not a soldier, shall be deemed guilty of having made a false muster, and shall suffer accordingly.

ART. 13. Any officer who shall, knowingly, make a false return to the department of war, or to any of his superior officers, authorised to call for such returns of the state of the regiment, troop, company, or garrison, under his command, or of the arms, ammunition, and clothing or other stores thereunto belonging, shall, on conviction thereof before a court martial, be cashiered.

ART. 14. The commanding officer of every regiment, troop, or independent company, or garrison of the republic, shall, in the beginning of every month, remit, through the proper channels, to the department of war, an exact return of the regiment, troop, independent company, or garrison, under his command, specifying the names of the officers then absent from their posts, with the reasons for, and the time of their absence. And any officer who shall he convicted of having, through neglect or design, omitted sending such returns, shall be punished according to the nature of the offence, by the sentence of a general court martial.

ART. 15. All officers and soldiers who have received pay, or have been duly enlisted in the service of the republic, and shall be convicted of having deserted the same, shall suffer death, or other punishment, as by sentence of a court martial shall be decreed.

ART. 16. Any non-commissioned officer, or soldier, who shall, without leave from his commanding officer, absent himself from his troop, company, or detachment, shall, upon being convicted thereof, be punished according to the nature of his offence, at the discretion of a court martial. No non-commissioned officer, or soldier, shall enlist himself in any other regiment, troop, or company, without a regular discharge from the regiment, troop, or company in which he last served, on the penalty of being reputed a deserter, and suffering accordingly; and in case any officer shall, knowingly, receive or entertain such non-commissioned officer, or soldier, or who shall not, after his being discovered to be a deserter, confine him, and give notice thereof to the corps in which he has served, the said officer shall, by a court martial, be cashiered.

ART. 17. Any officer, or soldier, who shall be convicted of having advised or persuaded any other officer or soldier to desert the service of the republic, shall suffer death, or such other punishment as shall be inflicted upon him by the sentence of a court martial.

ART. 18. No officer or soldier shall use any reproachful language or gesture to another; if an officer, upon pain of being put under arrest; if a soldier, confined; and shall ask pardon of the party offended in the presence of the commanding officer.

ART. 19. No officer or soldier shall send a challenge to another officer or soldier to fight a duel, or accept a challenge if sent, upon pain, if a commissioned officer, of being cashiered; if a non-commissioned officer or soldier, of suffering corporeal punishment, at the discretion of a court martial.

ART. 20. If any commissioned or non-commissioned officer of a guard shall, knowingly or willingly, suffer any person whatever to go forth to fight a duel, he shall be punished as a challenger; and all seconds, promoters, and carriers of challenges, in order to fight a duel, shall be deemed as principals, and punished accordingly. And it shall be the duty of every officer commanding an army, regiment, post, or detachment, who is knowing to a challenge being given to, or accepted by any officer, non-commissioned officer, or soldier under his command, or has reason to believe the same to be the case, immediately to bring to trial such offenders.

ART. 21. All officers, of what condition soever, have power to part and quell all quarrels, frays, and disorders, though the person concerned shall belong to another regiment, troop, or company, and either to order officers into arrest, non-commissioned officers and soldiers into confinement, until their proper superior officers shall be acquainted therewith; and whoever shall refuse to obey such officer, (though of inferior rank) or shall draw his sword upon him, shall be punished at the discretion of a general court martial.

ART. 22. Any officer, or soldier, who shall upbraid another for refusing a challenge, shall himself be punished as a challenger; and all officers and soldiers are hereby discharged from any imputation of dishonor or disgrace, which might arise from their having refused to accept of challenges, as they will only have acted in obedience to the laws, and done their duties as good soldiers, who subject themselves to discipline.

ART. 23. All officers, commanding in the field, forts, barracks, or garrisons of the republic, are hereby required to see that all the persons permitted to settle, shall supply the soldiers with good and wholesome provisions, or other articles, at a reasonable price, as they shall be answerable for their neglect.

ART. 24. No person commanding in any of the forts, garrisons, or barracks of the republic, shall exact exorbitant prices, for houses, stalls let out to settlers, or connive at the like exactions in others, or by his own authority, or for his private advantage, lay any duty or imposition, or be interested in the sale of any victuals, liquors, or other necessaries of life brought into the forts, garrisons, and barracks, for the use of the soldiers, on the penalty of being discharged from the service.

ART. 25. Every officer commanding in quarters, garrison, or on the march, shall keep good order, and to the utmost of his ability, redress all abuses or disorders, which may be committed by any officer or soldier under his command, if upon complaint made to him, of officers or soldiers beating, or otherwise ill treating any person; of disturbing fairs and markets, or of committing any kind of riot, to the disquiet of the citizens of this republic, he, the said commander, who shall refuse or omit to see justice done to the offender or offenders, and reparation made to the party or persons injured, as far as part of the offender's pay shall enable him or them, shall, upon proof thereof, be cashiered, or otherwise punished as a general court martial shall direct.

ART. 26. When any commissioned officer or soldier shall be accused of a capital crime, or of having used violence, or committed any offence against the person or property of any citizen of the republic, such as is punishable by the known laws of the land, the commanding officer and officers of every regiment, troop, or company, to which the person or persons so accused shall belong, are hereby required, upon application duly made, by or in behalf of the party or parties so injured, to use their utmost endeavours to deliver over such accused person or persons to the civil magistrate, and likewise to be aiding and assisting to the officers of justice, in apprehending and securing the person or persons so accused, in order to bring him or them to trial. If any commanding officer, or officers, shall wilfully neglect or refuse, upon the application aforesaid, to deliver over such accused person or persons to the civil magistrates, or to be aiding and assisting to the officers of justice, in apprehending such person or persons, the officer or officers so offending, shall be cashiered.

ART. 27. If any officer shall think himself wronged by his colonel, or the commanding officer, and shall, upon due application being made to him, be refused redress, he may complain to the general commanding in the division or brigade to which his regiment is attached, in order to obtain justice; who is hereby required to examine into the said complaint, and take proper measures for redressing the wrongs complained of, and transmit as soon as possible to the department of war a true statement of said complaint, with the proceedings had thereon.

ART. 28. If any inferior officer or soldier shall think himself wronged by his captain or other officer, he is to complain thereof to the commanding officer of the regiment, who is hereby required to summon a regimental court martial for doing justice to the complainant: from which regimental court martial either party may, if he thinks himself still aggrieved, appeal to a general court martial; but if, upon a second hearing, the appeal shall appear vexatious and groundless, the person so appealing shall be punished at the discretion of the said court martial.

ART. 29. Any commissioned officer, store keeper, or commissary, who shall be convicted, at a general court martial, of having sold, without a proper order for that purpose, embezzled, misapplied, or wilfully or through neglect, suffer any of the provisions, arms, forage, clothing, or other military stores, belonging to the republic, to be spoiled or damaged, shall at his own expense make good the damages; and shall, moreover, forfeit all his pay and be dismissed from the service.

ART. 30. Any non-commissioned officer or soldier, who shall be convicted at a general court martial, of having sold, lost, or spoiled, through neglect, his horse, arms, clothes or accoutrements, shall undergo such weekly stoppages (not exceeding half of his pay) as such court martial shall judge sufficient for repairing the loss or damage, and shall suffer confinement or such corporeal punishment as his crime shall deserve.

ART. 31. Any non-commissioned officer or soldier who shall be convicted at a regimental court martial, of having sold, or designedly, or through neglect, wasted the ammunition delivered out to him, to be employed in the service of the republic, shall be punished at the discretion of such court.

ART. 32. Every officer who shall be convicted, before a court martial, of having embezzled or misapplied any money with which he may have been entrusted, for the payment of the men under his command, or for enlisting men into the service, or for other purposes, if a commissioned officer, shall be cashiered, and compelled to refund the money; if a non-commissioned officer, shall be reduced to the ranks, be put under stoppages until the money be made good, and suffer such corporeal punishment as such court martial shall direct.

ART. 33. Every captain of a company is charged with the arms and accoutrements, ammunition, clothing, or other warlike stores, belonging to the troop or company under his command, which he is to he accountable for to his colonel, in case of their being lost, spoiled and damaged, not by unavoidable accidents, or on actual service.

ART. 34. No officer or soldier shall be out of his quarters, garrison, or camp, without leave from the superior officer, upon penalty of bring punished according to the nature of his offence, by the sentence of a court martial.

ART. 35. Every non-commissioned officer and soldier shall retire to his quarters or tent at the beating of retreat, in default of which he shall be punished according to the nature of his offence, by the sentence of a court martial.

ART. 36. No officer, non-commissioned officer, or soldier, shall fail in repairing to the place of parade, of exercise, or other rendezvous, appointed by his commanding officer, if not prevented by sickness or some other evident necessity, or shall go from the said place of rendezvous without leave from his commanding officer, before he shall be regularly relieved or dismissed, on the penalty of being punished according to the nature of his offence, by the sentence of a court martial.

ART. 37. Any commissioned officer who shall be found drunk on his post, shall be cashiered. Any non-commissioned officer or soldier so offending, shall suffer such corporeal punishment as shall be inflicted by the sentence of a court martial.

ART. 38. Any sentinel who shall be found sleeping upon his post, or shall leave it before he shall be regularly relieved, shall suffer death, or such other punishment as shall be inflicted by the sentence of a court martial.

ART. 39. No soldier belonging to any regiment, troop, or company, shall hire another to do his duty for him, or be excused from duty, but in case of sickness, disability, or leave of absence and every soldier found guilty of hiring his duty, as also the party so hired to do another's duty, shall be punished at the discretion of a regimental court martial.

ART. 40. And every non-commissioned officer conniving at such hiring of duty aforesaid shall be reduced; and every commissioned officer knowing and allowing such ill practices in the service, shall be punished by the sentence of a general court martial.

ART. 41. Any officer belonging to the service of the republic, who, by firing of arms, drawing of swords, beating of drums, or by any other means whatsoever, shall occasion false alarms in camp, garrison, or quarters, shall suffer death, or such other punishment as shall be ordered by the sentence of a general court martial.

ART. 42. Any officer or soldier who shall, without urgent necessity, or without the leave of his superior officers, quit his guard, platoon, or division, shall be punished according to the nature of his offence, by the sentence of a court martial.

ART. 43. No officer or soldier shall do violence to any person, who brings provisions or other necessaries to the camp, garrison, or quarters of the forces of the republic, employed in any part of the republic, upon pain of death or such other punishment as a court martial shall direct.

ART. 44. Any officer or soldier who shall misbehave himself before the enemy, runaway, or shamefully abandon any fort, post, or guard, which he or they may be commanded to defend, or speak words inducing others to do the crime, or shall cast away his arms and ammunition, or who shall quit his post, or colors, to plunder and pillage; every such offender, being duly convicted thereof, shall suffer death, or such other punishment as shall be ordered by the sentence of a general court martial.

ART. 45. Any person belonging to the armies of the republic, who shall make known the watchword to any person who is not entitled to receive it, according to the rules and discipline of war, or shall presume to give a parole or watchword different from what he received, shall suffer death, or such other punishment as shall be ordered by the sentence of a general court martial.

ART. 46. All officers and soldiers are to behave themselves orderly in quarters and upon the march; and whoever shall commit any waste or spoil, either in walks of trees, parks, warrens, fish ponds, houses and gardens, enclosures, cornfields, &c., or shall maliciously destroy any property whatsoever, belonging to the republic, unless by command of the commander-in-chief the armies of the said republic, shall (besides such penalties as they are subject to by law) be punished according to the nature and degree of the offence, by the judgment of a general or regimental court martial.

Whosoever employed in the armies of the republic in foreign parts, shall force a safeguard, shall suffer death.

ART. 47. Whosoever shall relieve the enemy with money, victuals, or ammunition, or who shall knowingly harbor or protect an enemy, shall suffer death, or such other punishment as shall be ordered by the sentence of a court martial.

ART. 48. Whosoever shall be convicted of holding a correspondence with, or giving intelligence to the enemy, either directly or indirectly, shall suffer death, or such other punishment as shall be ordered by the sentence of a court martial.

ART. 49. All public stores taken in the enemy's camp, towns, ports, or magazines, whether of artillery, ammunition, clothing, forage, or provisions, shall be secured for the service of the republic, for the neglect of which the commanding officer is to be answerable.

ART. 50. If any commander of any garrison, fortress, or post, shall be compelled, by the officers and soldiers under his command, to give up to the enemy, or abandon it, the commissioned officers or soldiers, who shall be convicted of having so offended, shall suffer death, or such other punishment as shall be inflicted upon them by the sentence of a court martial.

ART. 51. All suttlers and retainers to the camp, and persons whatsoever, serving with the armies of the republic in the field, though not enlisted soldiers, are to be subject to orders, according to the rules and discipline of war.

ART. 52. Officers having commissions of a prior date to those of the regiment in which they serve, may take place in courts martial and on detachments, when composed of different corps according to the rank given them in their former commissions; but in the regiment, troop, or company, to which such officers belong, they shall do duty and take rank, both in courts martial, and on detachments, which shall be composed only of their own corps, according to the commissions by which they are mustered in said company.

ART. 53. The functions of the engineers being generally confined to the most elevated branch of military science, they are not to assume, nor are they subject to be ordered on any duty beyond the line of their profession except by the special order of the president of the republic, but they are to receive every mark of respect to which their rank in the army may entitle them respectively, and are liable to be transferred at the pleasure of the president, from one corps to another, regard being had to rank.

ART. 54. General courts martial may consist of any number of commissioned officers, from five to thirteen, inclusive, but they shall not consist of less than thirteen, when that number can be convened without manifest injury to the service.

ART. 55. Any general officer commanding an army, or colonel commanding a separate department, may appoint general courts martial whenever necessary. But no sentence of a court martial shall be carried into execution until after the whole proceedings shall have been laid before the officers ordering the same, or the officer commanding the troops for the time being; neither shall any sentence of a general court martial in time of peace, extending to the loss of life, dismission of a commissioned officer, or which in a time of peace or war, respecting a general officer, be carried into execution until after the whole proceedings shall have been transmitted to the secretary of war, to be laid before the president of the republic for his confirmation or disapproval; and orders in the case of all other sentences may be confirmed and executed by the officer ordering the court to assemble, or the commanding officer for the time being, as the case may be.

ART. 56. Whenever a general officer commanding an army, or a colonel commanding a separate detachment, shall be the prosecutor or accuser of any officer in the army of the republic, under his command, the general court martial for the trial of such officer shall be appointed by the president of the republic.

ART. 57. The proceedings and sentence of said court shall be sent directly to the secretary of war, to be by him laid before the president for his confirmation or approval, or orders in the case.

ART. 58. Every officer commanding a regiment or corps may appoint courts martial, to consist of three commissioned officers for the trial and punishment of offences not capital, and decide upon their sentences. For the same purposes, all officers commanding any garrisons, forts, barracks, and other places when the troops consist of different corps, and in cases wherein there is but one corps, and the commanding officer, not authorized to order a regimental court martial, may assemble courts martial to consist of three commissioned officers, and decide upon their sentences.

ART. 59. No garrison or regimental court martial shall have power to try capital cases or commissioned officers, neither shall they inflict a fine exceeding one month's pay, nor imprison nor put to hard labor, any non-commissioned officer or soldier for a longer time than one month.

ART. 60. The judge advocate, or some person deputed by him, or by the general, or officer commanding the army, detachment, or garrison, shall prosecute in the name of the republic, but shall so far consider himself as counsel for the prisoner, after the said prisoner shall have made his plea, as to object to any leading question, to any of the witnesses, or to the prisoner, the answer to which might tend to criminate himself; and administer to each member of the court, before they proceed to any trial, the following oath, which shall also be taken by all members of the garrison and regimental courts martial:

"You   do solemnly swear that you will well and truly try, and determine according to evidence, the matter now before you, between the republic of Texas and the prisoner to be tried, and that you will truly administer justice according to an act establishing rules and articles for the government of the armies of the republic of Texas, without favor, partiality, or affection; and if any doubts shall arise, not explained by said articles according to your conscience, the best of your understanding, and the custom of war in like cases; and you do further swear, that you will not divulge the sentence of the court martial, until it shall be published by the proper authority; neither will you discover or disclose the vote or the opinion of any particular members of this court martial, unless required to give evidence thereof, as a witness, by a court of justice, in due course of law, so help you God."

And so soon as the said oath shall have been administered to the respective members, the president of the court shall administer to the judge advocate, or person officiating as such, an oath in the following words:

"You   do solemnly swear that you will not disclose or discover the vote or opinion of any member of the court martial, unless required to give evidence thereof as a witness by a court of justice, in the course of law, nor divulge the sentence of the court, to any but the proper authority, until it shall be duly disclosed by the same; so help you God."

ART. 61. When a prisoner, arraigned before a general court martial, shall, from obstinacy and deliberate design, stand mute, or answer foreign to the purpose, the court may proceed to trial and judgment, as if the prisoner had regularly pleaded not guilty.

ART. 62. When a member shall be challenged by a prisoner, he must state his cause of challenge of which the court shall, after due deliberation, determine the validity or relevancy, and decide accordingly; and no challenge to more than one member at a time, shall be received by the court.

ART. 63. All numbers of a court martial are to behave with decency

decency and calmness, and in giving their votes shall begin with the youngest in commission.

ART. 64. All persons who give evidence before a court martial are to be examined on oath or affirmation, in the following form: "You swear or affirm (as the case may be) the evidence you shall give, in the case now in hearing, shall be the truth, the whole truth, and nothing but the truth, so help me God."

ART. 65. On the trials of cases, not capital, before courts martial, the deposition of witnesses, not in line or staff of the army, may be taken before some justice of the peace, and read in evidence, provided the prosecutor and person accused are present on taking the same, or are duly notified thereof.

ART. 66. No officer shall be tried by a general court martial, nor by officers of an inferior rank, if it can be avoided; nor shall any proceedings or trials be carried on, excepting between the hours of eight in the morning and three in the afternoon, excepting in cases which, in the opinion of the officers appointed, the court martial required immediate example.

ART. 67. No person whatsoever shall use any name, any gestures, or sign in presence of a court martial, or shall cause any disorder or riot, or disturb then proceedings, in the penalty of being punished at the discretion of said court martial.

ART. 68. No officer shall be tried but by a general court martial, or shall cause any disorder or riot or disturb their proceedings, on the penalty of being punished at the discretion of a court martial.

ART. 69. Whenever any officer shall be charged with a crime, he shall be confined to his barracks, quarters, or tent, and deprived of his sword, by the commanding officer; and any officer who shall leave his confinement before he shall be set at liberty by his commanding officer, or by a superior officer, shall be cashiered. Non-commissioned officers and privates charged with crimes, shall be confined and tried by a court martial, or released by a proper authority.

ART. 70. No officer or soldier who shall be put in arrest shall continue in confinement more than eight days, or such time as a court martial can be assembled.

ART. 71. No officer commanding any guard, or provost martial shall refuse to receive or keep any prisoners committed to his charge by any officer belonging to the forces of the republic, provided the officer at the same time deliver an account in writing, signed by himself, of the crime with which the said prisoner is charged.

ART. 72. No officer commanding a guard, or provost martial shall presume to release any person committed to his charge without authority for so doing, nor shall he suffer any person to escape in the penalty of being punished for it by a court martial.

ART. 73. Every officer or provost martial, to whose charge prisoners shall be committed, shall, within twenty-four hours after such commitment, or as soon as he shall be relieved from his guard, make report in writing, to the commanding officer of their names, their crimes, and the names of the officers who committed them, on the penalty of being punished for disobedience or neglect, at the discretion of a court martial.

ART. 74. Any commissioned officer convicted before a general court martial, of conduct unbecoming an officer and a gentlemen, shall be dismissed the service.

ART. 75. In cases when a court martial may think it proper to sentence a commissioned officer to be suspended from command, they shall have power also to suspend his pay and emoluments for the same time, according to the nature and heinousness of the offence.

ART. 76. In all cases, when a commissioned officer is cashiered for cowardice or fraud, it shall be added in the sentence, that the crime, name and place of abode, and punishment of the delinquent, be published in the newspapers, in and about the camp, or where he usually resides, after which it shall be deemed scandalous for an officer to associate with him.

ART. 77. The commanding officer of any post or detachment, in which there shall not be a number of officers adequate to form a general court martial, shall, in cases which require the cognizance of such a court, report to the commanding officer of the department, who shall order a court to be assembled at the nearest post or detachment, and the party accused, with the necessary witnesses, to be transported to the place where the said court shall be assembled.

ART. 78. No person shall be sentenced to suffer death but by the concurrence of two thirds of the members of a general court martial, nor except in cases herein expressly mentioned; nor shall more than fifty lashes be inflicted on any offender at the discretion of a court martial; and no officer, non-commissioned officer or soldier, or follower of the army, shall be tried a second time for the same offence.

ART. 79. No person shall be liable to be tried and punished by a general court martial for any offence that shall appear to have been committed more than two years before the issuing of the order for such trial, unless the person, by reason of having absented himself, or some other manifest impediment, shall not have been amenable to justice within that period.

ART. 80. Every officer authorized to order a general court martial, shall have power to pardon or mitigate any punishment ordered by such court, except the sentence of death, or of cashiering an officer, which in the cases he has authority (by Article 65) to carry them into execution, he may suspend, until the pleasure of the president of the republic of Texas can be known; which suspension, together with copies of the proceedings of the court martial, the said officer shall immediately transmit to the president for his determination; and the colonel or commanding officer of the regiment or garrison, where any regimental or garrison court martial shall be held, may pardon or mitigate any punishment ordered by such court to be inflicted.

ART. 81. Every judge advocate, or person officiating as such, at any general court martial, shall transmit, with as much expedition as the opportunity of time and distance of place can admit, the original proceedings and sentence of such court martial, to the secretary of war; which said original proceedings and sentence, shall be carefully kept, and preserved in the office of said secretary, and that the persons entitled thereto, may be enabled, upon application to the said office, to obtain copies thereof.

ART. 82. The party tried by any general court martial, shall, upon demand thereof, made by himself, or by any person or persons in his behalf, be entitled to a copy of the sentence and proceedings of such court martial.

ART. 83. In eases when the general or commanding offices may order a court of inquiry to examine into the nature of any transaction, accusation or imputation against any officer or soldier, the said court shall consist of one or more officers not exceeding three, and a judge advocate or other suitable person, as recorder, to reduce the proceedings and evidence to writing, all of whom shall be sworn to the faithful performance of their duty. This court shall have the same power to summon witnesses for a court martial, and to examine them on oath; but they shall not give their opinion on the merits of the case, excepting they shall be thereto specially required. The parties accused shall also be permitted to cross examine and interrogate the witnesses, so as to investigate fully the circumstances in the question.

ART. 84. The proceedings of a court of inquiry must be authenticated by the signatures of the recorder and the president, and delivered to the commanding officer; and the said proceedings may be admitted as evidence by a court martial, in cases not capital, or extending to the dismission of an officer, provided that the circumstances are such that real testimony cannot be obtained. But as courts of inquiry may be perverted to dishonorable purposes, and may be considered as engines of destruction to military merit, in the hands of weak and envious commandants, they are hereby prohibited, unless directed by the president of the republic, or demanded by the accused.

ART. 85. The judge advocate or recorder shall administer to the members the following oath: "You shall well and truly examine and enquire, according to your evidence, into the matter now before you, without favour, partiality, affection, prejudice, or hope of reward, so help you God."

ART. 86. After which the president shall administer to the judge advocate or recorder the following oath: "You do solemnly swear that you will, according to your best abilities, accurately and impartially record the proceedings and the evidence to be given in the case in hearing, so help you God." The witnesses shall take the same oath as witnesses sworn before court martial.

ART. 87. When any commissioned officer shall die, or be killed in the service of the republic, the major of the regiment, or the officer doing the major's duty in his absence, or in post or garrison, the second officer in command, or the assistant military agent, shall immediately secure all his effects or equipage then in camp or quarters, and shall make an inventory thereof, and forthwith transmit the same to the officer of the department of war, to the end that his executors or administrators may receive the same.

ART. 88. When any non-commissioned officer or soldier shall die, or be killed in the service of the republic, the then commanding officer of the troops or company shall, in the presence of two other commissioned officers, take an account of what effects he died possessed of, above his arms and accoutrements, and transmit the same to the department of war; which said effects are to be accounted for, and paid to the representative of such deceased non-commissioned officer or soldier; and in case any of the officers so authorized to take care of the effects of deceased officers and soldiers, should, before they have accounted to the representatives of the same, have occasion to leave the regiment or post, by preferment or otherwise, they shall, before they be permitted to quit the same, deposit in the hands of the commanding officer, or of the assistant military agent, all the effects of such deceased non-commissioned officers and soldiers, in order that the same may be secured and paid to their respective representatives.

ART. 89. All officers, conductors, gunners, matrosses, drivers, or other persons whatsoever, receiving pay or hire in the corps of artillery, or engineers of the republic, shall be governed by the aforesaid rules and articles, and shall be subject to be tried by courts martial, in like manner with the officers and soldiers of the other troops in the service of the republic.

ART. 90. The officers and soldiers of any troops, whether militia or others, being mustered and in pay of the republic, shall at all times and in all places, when joined or acting in conjunction with the regular forces of the republic, be governed by such rules and articles of war, and shall be subject to be tried by a court martial, in like manner with the officers and soldiers of the regular forces, save only that such courts martial shall be composed entirely of militia officers.

ART. 91. All crimes not capital, and all disorders and neglects, which officers and soldiers may be guilty of, to the prejudice of good order and military discipline, though not mentioned in the foregoing articles of war, are to be taken cognizance of by a general or regimental court martial, according to the nature and degree of the offence, and be punished at their discretion.

ART. 92. The president of the republic shall have power to prescribe the uniform of the army.

ART. 93. The foregoing are to be read and published once in every two months, to every garrison, regiment, troop, or company, mustered or to be mustered into the service of the republic, and are to be duly observed and obeyed by all officers and soldiers, who are or shall be in said service.

ART. 94. *And be it further enacted*, That in time of war, all persons not being citizens of, or owning allegiance to the republic, who shall be found lurking as spies in or about the fortifications or encampments of the republic, or any of them, shall suffer death, according to the law and usage of nations, by sentence of a court martial.

ART. 95. If any non-commissioned officer, musician, or private, shall desert the service of the republic, he shall, in addition to the penalties mentioned in the rules and articles of war, be liable to serve for and during such a period as shall, and may be tried by a court martial, and punished, although the terms of his enlistment may have elapsed previous to his being apprehended or tried.

ART. 96. Whenever a general court martial shall be ordered, the president of the republic may appoint some fit person to act as judge advocate; and in cases where the president shall not have made such appointment, the brigadier general, or the president of the court may make the same.

IRA INGRAM,
Speaker of the house of representatives.

MIRABEAU B. LAMAR,
President of the senate.

Approved Nov. 21, 1836.

SAM. HOUSTON.

————

JOINT RESOLUTION

For the relief of J. M. Wolf.

Resolved, by the senate and house of representatives of the republic of Texas, in congress assembled, That the secretary of the treasury is hereby authorized to pay (out of any money in the treasury not otherwise appropriated) the sum of fourteen hundred and two dollars and sixty-two cents, to Mr. J. M. Wolf, or to his legal representatives.

IRA INGRAM,
Speaker of the house of representatives.

RICHARD ELLIS,
President pro tem. of the senate.

Approved Nov. 30, 1836.

SAM. HOUSTON.

JOINT RESOLUTION

Prescribing oaths of office.

Be it resolved by the senate and house of representatives of the republic, of Texas, in congress assembled, That the following oaths of office, in addition to the oath prescribed by the constitution, be taken by the secretary of state, treasury, war, and navy, and chief clerks of the several departments, which several oaths shall be administered by the speaker of the house of representatives.

"I do solemnly swear (or affirm) that I will truly, honestly, and faithfully discharge the duties of   , without favor or partiality, to the best of my skill and ability. So help me God."

IRA INGRAM,
Speaker of the house of representatives.

RICHARD ELLIS,
President of the senate pro tem.

Approved Nov. 30, 1836.

SAM. HOUSTON.

JOINT RESOLUTION

Authorizing the president to reorganize the army.

SEC. 1. *Resolved by the senate and house of representatives of the republic of Texas in congress assembled,* That the president, of this republic be, and is hereby authorized to reorganize the army of Texas, in conformity with the regulations adopted by this government, and when such regulations are silent, in conformity with the military regulations of the United States of America.

SEC. 2. *Be it further resolved*, That all contingent military commissions heretofore granted to gentlemen, now in the United States, for the purpose of bringing men into our service, shall be confirmed in proportion to the respective number they may introduce by the tenth of January next, either for the term of two years or for during the war, to wit: for a second lieutenant twenty men, for a first lieutenant thirty men, for a captain fifty-six men, for a major two hundred and eighty men, for a lieutenant-colonel four hundred men, for a colonel five hundred and sixty men, and for a brigadier-general eleven hundred and twenty men.

IRA INGRAM,

Speaker of the house of representatives.

RICHARD ELLIS,

President pro tem. of the senate.

Approved Nov. 30, 1836.

SAM. HOUSTON.

AN ACT

To protect the Frontier.

SEC. 1. *Be it enacted by the senate and house of representatives of the republic of Texas, in congress assembled*, That the president be, and he is hereby required to raise, with as little delay as possible, a battalion of mounted riflemen, to consist of two hundred and eighty men, for the protection of the frontier, to be officered in like manner as the balance of the army.

SEC. 2. *Be it further enacted*, That the term of service of said corps shall be for twelve months or upwards, and each man shall be bound to furnish himself with a suitable, serviceable horse, a good rifle, and one brace of pistols, if they can be procured: and no one shall be allowed to enter said corps without first submitting his horse, arms, and equipments, to the inspection of an officer specially appointed by the inspector general of the army, who shall certify that such man, horse, and equipments are fit for the service.

SEC. 3. *Be it further enacted*, That the pay, emoluments, and bounty of said corps shall be same as that provided for other corps of the army, with this addition, that the sum of fifteen dollars per month be allowed for the furnishing of the horses and arms.

SEC. 4. *Be it further enacted*, That the president be, and he is hereby authorized to order out, for the protection of the frontier, such number of the militia as the exigencies of the case may require.

SEC. 5. *Be it further enacted*, That it shall be the duty of the president to cause to be erected such block houses, forts, and trading houses, as in his judgment may be necessary to prevent Indian depredations.

SEC. 6. *Be it further enacted*, That the president have full power, when in his opinion the exigencies of the country may require it, to order said corps to any other point than the frontier, or to the main army.

SEC. 7. *Be it further enacted*, That it shall be the duty of the president to enter into such negotiations and treaties as in his opinion may secure peace to the frontiers; and that he have power to appoint agents to reside amongst the Indians, and that he be authorized to distribute amongst the different tribes such presents as he may deem necessary, not to exceed in amount twenty thousand dollars.

SEC. 8. *Be it further enacted*, That the said corps shall be under the same rules, regulations, and restrictions of the regular army of this republic; and should any officer or soldier be found guilty of a wilful neglect of duty or disobedience of the orders of his superiors, he shall be subject to the usual pains and penalties inflicted on officers and soldiers in the regular army for like offences.

SEC. 9. *Be it further enacted*, That should a larger force be necessary, the president shall be authorized to extend the number so as not to exceed one regiment, or five hundred and sixty men, rank and file.

IRA INGRAM,
Speaker of the house of representatives.

RICHARD ELLIS,
President pro tem. of the Senate.

Approved Dec. 5, 1836.

SAM. HOUSTON.

LAWS

AN ACT

To provide for the national defence by organizing the Militia.

SEC. 1. *Be it enacted by the senate and house of representatives of the republic of Texas, in congress assembled*, That every free able bodied male citizen of this republic, resident therein, who is or shall be of the age of seventeen years, and under the age of fifty years, (except as hereinafter excepted) shall severally and respectively be enrolled in the militia, by the captain or commanding officer of the company, within whose bounds such citizens shall reside, and that within twenty days after receiving this act, with his commission and instructions. And it shall hereafter be the duty of such captain or commanding officer of a company, to enroll every such citizen as aforesaid, and all those who shall from time to time arrive at the age of seventeen years or being of the age of seventeen years and under the age of fifty years, (except as before excepted) shall come to reside within his bounds; and shall within ten days notify such citizen of said enrollment, by a proper con-commissioned officer of said company, by whom such notice may be proved. That every citizen so enrolled and notified, shall within ten days thereafter provide himself with a good musket, a sufficient bayonet and belt, six flints, knapsack and cartridge box, with twenty-four suitable ball cartridges; or with a good rifle, yauger, or shot gun, knapsack, shot pouch, powder horn, fifty balls suitable to the calibre of his gun, and a half pound of powder, and shall appear so armed, accoutred and provided, when called out to exercise, or in service; and that said arms, ammunition, and accoutrements, belonging to a citizen so enrolled, shall be exempt from all suits, seizures, or sales.

SEC. 2. *Be it further enacted*, That the vice president of this republic, the officers, judicial and executive; the members of both houses of congress, and their officers; all custom house officers, with their clerks; all post musters, and those employed in carrying the mail; all ferrymen employed at any ferry on the public road; all pilots; all mariners actually employed in the sea service; and all persons who are now or may be hereafter exempted by law, shall be and are hereby exempted from militia duty.

SEC. 3. *Be it further enacted*, That the enrolled militia shall be laid off in divisions, brigades, regiments, battalions, and companies. The divisions, brigades, and regiments shall be laid off by the president, and subject to such changes as he may from time to time deem expedient. Each division shall consist of two brigades, each brigade of two regiments, each regiment of two battalions, each battalion of five companies, each company of sixty-four men rank and file; and that said divisions, brigades, and regiments be numbered at the formation thereof, and a record made of such numbers in the adjutant general's office; and when in the field or in the service of the republic, each division, brigade, and regiment, shall respectively take rank according to their numbers, reckoning the first in number highest in rank.

SEC. 4. *Be it further enacted*, That the said militia shall be officered as follows: To each division, one major general, to be elected by the field officers of his division; and two aids-de-camp, with rank of major, to be appointed by the said major general. To each brigade, one brigadier general, to be elected by the commissioned officers of his brigade; with one brigade inspector, to serve also as brigade major, with the rank of major; one aid-de-camp, with the rank of captain, to be appointed by said brigadier general. To each regiment, one colonel, one lieutenant colonel, and one major, to be elected by the members of said regiment; and to each company, one captain, two lieutenants, four sergeants, four corporals, one drummer, and one fifer or bugler; that the captains and lieutenants of each company shall be elected by the members of their respective companies; and that the non-commissioned officers and musicians be appointed by the captains of their respective companies. That there shall be for each regiment, a regimental staff, to consist of one adjutant and one quarter master, to rank as lieutenants; one pay master, one surgeon and assistant surgeon, one sergeant major, one drum major, and one fife major, to be appointed by the colonel of the same.

SEC. 5. *Be it further enacted*, That it shall be the duty of each major general, upon good cause shown, to order a division court martial for the trial of general staff and field officers; and when the trial is complete, he shall approve or disapprove of the proceedings thereof. He shall receive copies of returns from the majors of brigades, of their annual reports made to the adjutant general; and shall receive from the adjutant general copies of requisitions of men, made by by government upon his division. He shall, upon notice of invasion or insurrection, embody as many militia as he may think adequate to the emergency, notifying in the speediest manner to the president, whose directions and orders he shall obey. Whenever the major general may choose, he may attend at any muster or review whatsoever, and give any orders for disciplining the troops that he may deem expedient.

SEC. 6. *Be it further enacted*, That it shall be the duty of the brigadier general to appoint the time of regimental and battalion musters, for the year in which they are to fall; a written notice of which shall be delivered to the commanding officers of regiments, on or before the first day of March in every year. He shall give orders to summon brigade courts martial, and appoint the time and place for their sitting. He shall receive the proceedings of the said courts, and approve or disapprove of the sentence thereof. It is his especial duly to receive and sign the annual returns made by his brigade major; to visit each regiment in his brigade, at least once in a year, on their regimental muster days, and review them; and whenever he may be present at any muster in his brigade, to order the training and exercise thereof, if the occasion, in his opinion, shall require it.

SEC. 7. *Be it further enacted*, That the commandants of regiments shall receive the written orders of his general of brigade, for the times of holding regimental and battalion musters for the whole year, and shall give a notice in writing thereof to the commandants of battalions, on or before the first day of March in the year in which they are to fall. It shall be his duty to attend the regimental and battalion musters and reviews; to exercise his regiment himself on all review days; to superintend and correct the exercise of the battalion musters, and the company musters when he may choose so to do. It shall be his duty, at least once in a year, to receive the returns of commandants of battalions, and after examining and comparing them with the returns of the preceding year, and noting any casualties that may have occurred, he shall sign them in his official capacity, and return them to the major of brigade. Upon his receiving notice of invasion and insurrection, it shall be his duty immediately to embody such force as he may deem competent for the emergency, and give the earliest information thereof to the general of division or brigade. And it shall be his duty to convene the members of his regiment, to elect proper persons to fill vacancies therein; and he may receive the resignation of any subordinate officer in his regiment, and shall appoint regimental courts martial for the trial of officers within their cognizance, of which the commandant of the regiment shall approve or disapprove.

SEC. 8. *Be it further enacted*, It shall be the duty of commandants of battalions to receive the written orders of the commandants of regiments, for the days on which the regimental and battalion musters shall be appointed for the year, and give a written notice thereof to the commandants of companies, within their respective battalions, on or before the last day of March in every year. They shall exercise their battalions on their respective days of muster, and when they may be present at a company muster, they may superintend their exercise if they think proper. They shall receive, examine, and sign officially, the returns from the commanding officers of companies, which they shall comprise in a return of their battalion, and noting any difference that may have occurred, return them to the adjutant of the regiment, in conformity to their orders. They shall strictly examine the arms, ammunition, and accoutrements of the corps of companies composing their battalions, at their several musters, and shall see that their enrolments and classifications are correct and according to law.

SEC. 9. *Be it further enacted*, That the commanding officers of battalions shall give to those commanding companies, a written notice of the days on which the regimental and battalion musters shall fall during that year; to which the said commandants of companies shall add the days appointed for the muster of their companies for the same year; and he shall deliver within five days afterwards, to wit, by the fifth day of April in every year, a certificate of the musters so ordered, to the sergeant, whose duty it shall be to deliver it, or leave it at the abode of each corporal, musician, and private in the company to which he belongs, a like written notice, on or before the fifth day of April in each year. Each commandant of a company shall lay off his men into ten classes, for an equal routine of duty, and when called upon, he shall begin with the first. He shall be observant in enrolling all the men within his bounds, comprising all who may, from time to time, settle or inhabit therein, for the space of ten days. It shall be the duty of the commandant to exercise his company at each of the musters thereof, agreeably to the rules prescribed by congress; to inspect their arms, &c., and to make an annual return thereof, agreeably to the form he may receive, which shall be officially. In every case the commandants of companies shall receive and execute the orders of his superior officers, and conform himself to such military regulations as the service may require.

SEC. 10. *Be it further enacted*, That all lieutenants, and other subordinate officers of companies, shall be obedient to and execute the official orders of their commandant. They are, in particular, to assist in the exercise and organization of their companies, and report every defalcation or disobedience in the government and exercise thereof.

SEC. 11. *Be it further enacted*, That so much of this law as relates to regimental and battalion musters, shall not require the militia to attend musters without the counties in which they live; but where counties shall not compose a regiment, a battalion muster only shall be required; and where a county shall not compose a battalion, a company muster shall only be required; provided that these musters shall be in the stead of the regimental musters, and additional to the usual company musters.

SEC. 12. *Be it further enacted*, That it shall be the duty of the president, forthwith to appoint one captain and two lieutenants for each county; and that it shall be the duty of the captain and lieutenants so appointed, within thirty days after their reception of their commissions, and a copy of this act, to enroll all the citizens subject to militia duty within their counties, and to report a list of their names to the adjutant general and the president, accompanied with such remarks and suggestions in regard to the proper boundaries of the different regiments, battalions, companies, &c., and such other remarks as they may think calculated to promote the objects of this act; and that said captains and lieutenants, while so engaged in enrolling the citizens of their respective counties, shall receive three dollars per diem; and in case of their refusal to accept their commissions, or perform the duties assigned them, they shall incur the penalty of a fine of one hundred dollars for each and every offence so committed.

SEC. 13. *Be it further enacted*, That an adjutant general shall be appointed, with the rank of colonel, as other field officers; his office shall he kept at the seat of government. Aids-de-camp shall be commissioned by the president; their duty shall be to carry and execute the orders of the major or brigadier general to whom they are attached. The brigade inspector shall be commissioned by the president. An adjutant and quartermaster shall be commissioned by the president; it shall be their duty to obey the orders of the commandants of regiments. The regimental surgeon and assistant surgeon, the paymaster, the sergeants, drum and fife majors are to conform to, and implicitly obey the orders they receive from commandants of regiments. Judge advocates shall be appointed to the several courts martial hereafter ordered by said court. It shall be the duty of the judge advocate to take and keep safely a true statement of all proceedings, whether pleas, evidence or defence made before a court martial, a fair copy of which he shall make out and deliver to the president, or officer ordering such court within twenty days after their adjournment, and to prosecute for the government.

SEC. 14. *Be it further enacted*, That courts martial shall be appointed for the trial of all offences arising from neglect of duty, disobedience of orders, or disorderly and ungentlemanly behavior. The president shall order general courts martial when he may think it necessary, where a major general shall preside, and be composed of eight additional members, two of whom shall be brigadiers, and the other six field officers. The proceedings of this court shall be approved by the president, from whose decision there can be no appeal. Division courts martial may be appointed at the discretion of the major general, where a brigadier shall preside, who, with six field officers, shall compose the court, whose proceedings shall be approved or disapproved, and whose sentence shall be affirmed or reversed by the major general who ordered such court, subject however (upon an appeal to the president) to his final affirmance or reversal. Brigade courts martial may be appointed at the discretion of the brigadiers general, where a colonel shall preside, who, with six additional officers, to wit, two field officers and four captains at least, shall compose such court, whose proceedings shall be approved by the brigadier general ordering it; subject, however, (upon an appeal to the president) to his final affirmance or reversal. Regimental courts martial shall be appointed by commandants of regiments, where a field officer shall preside, who, with six other regimental commissioned officers, two of whom at least shall be captains, shall compose a court for the trial of all officers below the grade of a field officer and the regimental staff, whose proceedings shall be approved or disapproved of by the commanding officer of the regiment; subject, however, to an appeal to the commandant of the brigade, for a final decision. In the general court martial, none shall be tried below the grade of a general officer or the general staff—in the division court martial, none shall be tried below the grade of a field officer—and in the brigade court martial, the field officers and brigade staff may be tried, or a captain, for good cause shown. Upon the convening of either of the courts herein directed, the president thereof shall administer to the judge advocate the following oath or affirmation: "I   do solemnly swear (or affirm as the case may be) that I will truly and faithfully execute the office of judge advocate to this court so long as I remain in office, to the best of my abilities and the laws of this republic; and that I will not disclose, or discover the opinion of any particular member of this court martial I act with, unless required to give evidence in a court of justice;" which oath shall be deemed a competent qualification to such judge advocate while he continues to act; and the judge advocate shall proceed to qualify the members, by administering the following oath: "You and each of you, do swear (or affirm) that you will well and truly try and determine, according to evidence, agreeably to justice, the best of your understanding, and the laws governing the case, between the republic of Texas and the prisoner to be tried; and you will not disclose the opinions of this court martial, where secrecy may be required, until made public by the proper officer; nor will you, at any time, disclose the vote or opinion of any particular member of this court martial, unless called upon by a court of justice to give evidence." Whereupon the court shall proceed to the business laid before them, and adjourn from day to day, until it is finished; of all of which a complete record shall be made, and signed by the president and judge advocate or recorder, and the court shall be dissolved. Upon the disclosure of the opinion or sentence of any court martial, any person may, according to this act, appeal therefrom, by filing a written notice with the officer to whom the appeal is made, within thirty days after the sentence is published; whose duty it shall be, to order up before him, the proceedings of such court for a final decision. Any officer, who shall have cause of complaint against his superior officer, shall file with the president, major general, brigadier general, or commandant of a regiment, the charges, certified in form, upon which an inquiry, or arrest, at discretion of such superior officer, may be awarded: *provided*, that from the commencement of an arrest, a court martial shall be ordered to meet within thirty days, of the time and place of which the officer arrested shall have at least twenty days notice. *And provided also*, that if, upon the meeting of such court, it shall appear that from the absence of witnesses, inability or sickness of the parties, or for any good cause shown, a fair and impartial trial could not then be had, they may adjourn the court to a future day, not exceeding six months. A court for assessment of fines, and receiving the returns of delinquents, shall be held on the last Monday of November in every year; a field officer of the regiment for which they are held shall preside; who, with four captains, four subalterns, the regimental judge advocate, and an orderly sergeant, may proceed to business; but every commissioned officer in the regiment shall be considered a member of the court ex-officio. This court is to examine all returns laid before them; to have the delinquents called, to show cause why judgment should not be awarded against them, and to deliver the opinions of the court, in every case, to the judge advocate, who is hereby directed to make a fair record thereof. This court shall also have the power of excusing from military duty, aged and disabled persons during their disability, and to hear evidence, and to determine the same. This court shall have power to adjourn from day to day, to compel the attendance of absent members, and when their business is completed, the president and judge advocate shall sign the record of their proceedings, and the court for that year shall be dissolved: *provided*, that previous to their proceeding to do any business whatever, the members and judge advocate composing the said court, take the following oath or affirmation, to wit: "We, and each of us, do swear (or affirm) that we will truly and diligently enquire into and decide upon the several delinquencies reported to us, and decide according to law and the best of our skill and understanding, without favor or the hope of reward." It shall be the duty of any officer resigning or removing, to deliver the list of public arms and laws that may be in his possession, to the commandant of the regiment at the time of his resignation or removal, who shall deliver the same to the successor of such officer.

SEC. 15. *Be it further enacted*, That there shall be, in the months of October or November in every year, regimental musters, at such places as the commandants may direct, where every field, staff, and regimental commissioned and non-commissioned officer, every private and musician shall attend. There shall be a battalion muster in every battalion, at such places as the commandants may direct, in the months of May and October in each year; each lieutenant colonel shall be commandant of the first battalion of his regiment, and the major of the second: where every officer, non-commissioned officer, and private shall attend. There shall be at least two company musters in each year, which shall be appointed at the discretion, as to time and place, of the commandants of companies, between the last day of May and the last day of November, where the commissioned, non-commissioned officers, musicians and privates of each company shall attend, armed and equipped according to law. At the several musters herein directed to be held, the troops shall be exercised at least three hours in each day, and no person present shall be exempt therefrom, except from sickness, or some sufficient cause; the rolls shall be called at each muster or review; and the delinquents particularly noted by the captains of companies, both as to absence, arms, accoutrements, and as to a failure and refusal to perform the duty required when present. Once in every year, on such days as the commanding officers of regiments shall appoint, the whole of the commissioned officers, non-commissioned officers, staff, and music belonging to a regiment, shall meet at the place for holding the musters and reviews thereof, equipped and armed in such manner as the commandant may direct, to be drilled and exercised by him, or under his direction, which exercise and drilling shall continue for three days in succession; at this muster the roll shall be called by the commandant, and the delinquents noted and returned as in other musters. At all musters and reviews, and attendance on courts martial, no persons are to give impediments or disturbance. Every officer and private shall be free from arrest (except for breaches of the peace or felony) whilst going to or returning from any review, muster, or court martial; and any person or persons, other than those performing military duty, who will wilfully impede or disturb any corps or court in their exercise or other duty, shall be apprehended by the commanding officer, kept under guard for three days, and fined not less than five dollars, nor more than one hundred dollars; the said sum to be paid over to the regimental paymaster. Returns shall be made by all officers commanding companies, to those commanding battalions, one every year at least, in which shall be expressed the strength of each company, and the number and kind of every sort of arms and equipments therein; whose duty it shall be to countersign them digested into battalion returns, and deliver them to the officer commanding the regiment, who shall cause a like regimental return to be made out and signed by himself, delivered to the brigadier general: the brigadier general shall cause the brigade inspector to digest the whole regimental into one general brigade return; which shall be signed by the brigadier or officer commanding the brigade, and transmitted to the adjutant general, whose duty it shall he to have all such returns recorded in a book to be kept for that purpose. The general of brigade shall, without delay, have a copy of such return made out by the brigade inspector, and sent to the major general or officer commanding the division. The brigade inspectors, adjutants of regiments, and commanding officers of companies, shall keep books, in which all returns shall be duly recorded, and the casual occurrences noted. On or before the fifteenth day of July in each year, the adjutants of regiments shall receive from the commanding officers, the returns of delinquents for that year, who shall record, and deliver them to the regimental judge advocates at least five days before the sitting of the court for the assessment of fines, in order that he may lay them before that body for adjudication. After the sitting of every court of assessment, the judge advocate shall make out two fair copies of their proceedings, one of which he shall deliver to the regimental paymasters, and the other to the brigade general; both of whom shall cause the same to be recorded. The regimental paymaster shall, on or before the first day of February in each year deliver to the high sheriff in each county, who shall, under the penalty of fifty dollars, to be recovered by the paymaster in any court having competent jurisdiction thereof, receive and receipt for all lists and copies of judgments against all delinquents and defaulters, as adjudged by the said court of assessment, and take his receipt therefor; who shall thereupon apply for and receive the same, and levy therefor, as in other cases, if payment is withheld; for which the said sheriff shall receive the same fees and per centum as are allowed by law for the collection of the public revenue. On or before the first day of September in every year, the said sheriff shall settle with and pay over to the regimental paymaster, all sums collected by him as aforesaid, and return upon oath an account of all insolvents and delinquents; recovering his commission as aforesaid, taking the said paymaster's receipt therefor; an attested copy of which he shall, within thirty days thereafter, transmit to the general of brigade, and also have recorded in the court for the county in which he is sheriff; but in the case the said sheriff fail or refuse to pay and settle with the paymaster as aforesaid, the said paymaster may immediately proceed to recover the monies due from the said sheriff and his securities, in the same manner that monies are recovered by the counties against their public collector.— Any person aggrieved by any decision of any court of assessment, may make affidavit thereof, and lodge the same with the judge advocate before the first day of February in each year, who thereupon shall present the same at the succeeding annual term: whereupon such grievance shall be reheard and decided upon; and if the former judgment shall be affirmed, such applicant shall be charged with fifty per cent, thereon, all of which the judge advocate shall record. The regimental paymaster shall, before he acts as such, enter into bond with sufficient security, in the county court, to the president and his successors in office, in the sum of one thousand dollars, conditioned for the just fulfillment of all the duties herein required of him, which bond shall not be void on the first recovery, and he shall also take the following oath: "I do swear, that I will, as paymaster to regiment of militia, truly and honestly perform the said duty, and render a just account to the best of my knowledge, when called upon by the law or the proper authority." And it shall be the duty of the field officers of every regiment, to call upon and settle with the paymaster annually; and they shall record a return of such settlement in the court of their county, signed by themselves, at the next court after the close of such settlements and the clerk shall perform such service ex-officio, and shall also sign a duplicate thereof, which shall be transmitted to the brigadier general commanding the brigade, who shall cause the same to be entered of record by the brigade inspector. The monies collected and funded with the regimental paymaster shall be subject to orders drawn by the commandant of the regiment, for regimental purposes, and to the orders of the major or brigadier general for any purpose immediately affecting the interest of the regiment or corps from whose paymaster the sum is drawn; all which orders shall be regularly filed and preserved by the paymaster, as vouchers in his annual settlement, for all and every duty herein specified. The said paymaster shall receive and be entitled to ten per cent, per annum, on all sums actually received and paid away. It shall be the duty of the adjutant general to call for any returns judged necessary by the president; and to furnish to each brigade forms thereof: and in like manner every commandant of division, brigade, or corps, are to be implicitly obeyed, when they may think it necessary to call for returns of their respective commands. Every division, brigade, and regiment shall be kept fully officered; and rosters in each shall be prepared by the proper officer, by which the detail of duty shall be regulated.

SEC. 16. *And be it further enacted*, That the president for the time being, when he deems it necessary, shall call forth into the service of this republic, such a number of militia as he shall deem expedient; a tour of duty shall be estimated at three months; and, when employed in the service of the republic, no militia shall be compelled to serve more than two tours without discharge. The militia, when in service, shall be governed by the articles of war, and the rules and regulations adopted for the army of the republic, and receive the same pay and rations as said army. Whenever a new regiment shall be ordered by the president, the field officers composing it shall meet and lay off the district into bounds for the companies; but at no time shall a company consist of less than thirty-two privates, and if at any time a company shall be reduced to a less number, it shall be incorporated with the adjoining companies, while such disabilities exist. Every officer commissioned (under this law) by president shall be implicitly obeyed as such, and shall continue to hold his commission for the space of two years from the date of his commission, unless he removes from the district in which his command operates. All courts martial, and of assessment, shall issue summons for witnesses, who shall attend; the process may be served by any constable or sheriff, and if such witnesses shall not attend, without a good excuse, he shall be fined. The president or any field officer may subpoena witnesses previous to the sitting of the court, and it is hereby directed that the several courts possess competent powers to carry into execution the regulations granted or analogous to their institution. In all courts martial, any person to be tried may make objections to any member or members composing the said court (not exceeding three) peremptorily, and assign his reasons for objections to others; if they are such as to evince their propriety, another or other members shall be summoned ; otherwise the court shall be deemed competent except the peremptory challenge. Parents and guardians shall be accountable for fines of their children, wares, &c., who are under twenty-one years of age: and it is hereby declared to every officer, non-commissioned officer, musician, and private, that the duties herein directed, are to be specifically and positively performed; and that each and every delinquent, upon a failure therein, may be charged with disobedience of orders, neglect of duty, or disorderly and ungentlemanly behaviour.

That courts martial at the discretion of those directed, or whose duty it is to make inquiry, be ordered to sit on such charges; whose duty it shall be to cashier, dismiss from service, reprimand, or acquit those accused, and also to assess any fine herein imposed, either in addition to, or abstracted from any other punishment. The pay and reward, to the commissioned and staff officers, for duties arising under this act, shall be as follows:

To the brigade inspector, for his services, to be certified by the brigadiers general, and paid by warrants on the treasury, four dollars per day. To every division judge advocate, to be paid by the paymaster of the regiments composing the division, by order of the major general, four dollars per day. To the brigade judge advocate, to be paid by the paymaster of the regiment composing the brigade, by order of the brigadier general, two dollars per day. To the regimental judge advocate, to be paid by the regimental paymaster, by order of the commandant, two dollars per day. To the orderly sergeants attending any of the above courts to be paid in the same manner as the judge advocates are, two dollars per day. To the adjutants of regiments, to be paid by the regimental paymaster, by orders drawn by the commandants of regiments, four dollars per day. To each drum and fife major, to be paid by the paymaster of the regiment, by order of the commandant, four dollars per day. To all expresses despatched on military service, to be paid by warrants on the treasury, by certificate from a major general, brigadier general, or commandants of regiments, four dollars per day. The fines implicated under this act shall be, on every major general, who shall not perform the duty or duties required, shall pay a fine of two hundred and fifty dollars. For failing to perform a tour of duty when called on, one thousand dollars. Every brigadier general, for neglect of his duty, shall pay, for not appointing the musters in the manner herein directed, two hundred dollars; for failing to perform a tour of duty when called on, seven hundred and fifty dollars; for failing to make annual returns one hundred dollars; for failing to review his brigade, for each regiment, fifty dollars. Every commandant of a regiment, for not appointing the mustering place of his regiment, fifty dollars; for failing to perform a tour of duty when called on, five hundred dollars; for not giving notice of musters, one hundred and fifty dollars; for not attending a regimental muster, fifty dollars; for not attending drill musters, per day, twenty-five dollars; for not attending courts martial, twenty-five dollars. Every commandant of battalion, for neglect of duty shall pay, for failing to perform a tour of duty when called on, four hundred dollars; for not giving notice of musters, one hundred dollars; for not attending and exercising their battalions on their days of muster, fifty dollars; for not making annual returns, twenty dollars; for not attending courts martial, or assessment, twenty dollars; for not attending drill musters, per day, fifteen dollars. Every commandant of a company shall pay, for failing to enroll the militia within his bounds, two hundred dollars; for failing to perform a tour of duty when called on, three hundred dollars; for not giving due notice of the musters, twenty-five dollars; for not classing his company for duty, fifty dollars; for not attending and exercising his company at the several musters, for each failure, twenty-five dollars; for not making his annual returns, fifty dollars; for not making a return of delinquents, fifty dollars; for not attending courts martial and assessment, twenty-five dollars. The adjutant general shall pay, for every neglect of duty enjoined by law, the sum of one hundred dollars. Aids-de-camp shall be fined for any neglect of their duty, for each offence, one hundred dollars. The regimental adjutant, quartermaster, surgeon, assistant surgeon, and paymaster, shall forfeit and pay, for every neglect of duty assigned by law, twenty-five dollars. Each sergeant, drum, and fife major shall pay, for not attending each muster, ten dollars. Each sergeant shall pay, for not attending each muster, the sum of seven dollars and fifty cents; for not giving notice of musters and courts martial, twenty dollars. Every private who fails to appear at any muster shall, for each offence, pay five dollars. Any officer, who shall appear at any parade, and refuses to do the duty required of him, shall pay a fine of fifty dollars. Any non-commissioned officer, musician, or private, who attends any parade, and refuses to do the duty required of him, shall pay double the fine for non-attendance. Every non-commissioned officer or private, who attends the parade at any muster, and does not bring arms and accoutrements, shall be fined five dollars, unless it shall appear to the court of assessment that such private is unable to provide such arms. For failing to perform a tour of duty when called on, one hundred dollars.

IRA INGRAM,
Speaker of the house of representatives.
RICHARD ELLIS,
President pro tem. of the Senate.
Approved Dec. 6, 1836.
SAM. HOUSTON.

———

JOINT RESOLUTION

For the relief of William Bryan.

SEC. 1. *Be it resolved by the senate and house of representative of the republic of Texas, in congress assembled,* That the secretary of the treasury, under the direction of the president, be, and he is hereby authorized to pay, out of the first available means which may be at the disposal of this government, all the debts and lawful demands against this government, now owned by William Bryan, Esq., of New

Orleans, or for which the said Bryan is in any way liable, to any individual or individuals, for or on account of this government.

SEC. 2. *Be it further resolved*, That the president be, and he is hereby authorized to place in the hands of said William Bryan, Esq., and authorize him to sell a sufficient quantity of Land Scrip to pay all the demands named in the foregoing resolution, and that he instruct him to apply the proceeds of the sale of said scrip to that special purpose: *provided*, that said scrip shall not be sold at a less price than fifty cents per acre; and that the said Bryan be required to file, in the office of the secretary of the treasury, proper vouchers for all said debts.

IRA INGRAM,
Speaker of the house of representatives.
MIRABEAU B. LAMAR,
President of the senate.

Approved Dec. 6, 1836.

SAM. HOUSTON.

––––––––

AN ACT

Compensating officers of the civil list.

SEC. 1. *Be it enacted by the senate and house of representatives of the republic of Texas, in congress assembled*, That the following shall be the compensation allowed to the officers of the civil list:

President, with house furnished, ten thousand dollars.
Vice President, three thousand dollars.
Secretary of State, three thousand five hundred dollars.
Secretary of Treasury, three thousand five hundred dollars.
Secretary of War, three thousand five hundred dollars.
Secretary of Navy, three thousand five hundred dollars.
Attorney General, three thousand dollars.
Post Master General, two thousand dollars.
Commissioner General of the Land Office, three thousand dollars.
Chief Clerks of departments, one thousand five hundred dollars.
Treasurer, two thousand five hundred dollars.
Auditor, two thousand five hundred dollars.
Chief Justice, five thousand dollars.
Associate, or District Judges, three thousand dollars.

Members of Congress, per diem, five dollars.

Speaker of the House of Representatives, per diem, seven dollars.

President pro tem, of the Senate, while acting as such, per diem, seven dollars.

Mileage for members of congress, for every twenty-five miles going and coming, five dollars.

The members and officers of the Consultation that sat at San Felipe in October and November of the last year, shall receive the same compensation and mileage as the members and officers of the present congress.

Chief Clerks of both houses, per diem, six dollars.

Foreign Ministers, four thousand five hundred dollars outfit; five thousand dollars salary per annum.

Consuls, perquisites.

Secretary of Legation, two thousand dollars.

Assistant Clerks, per diem, six dollars.

Reporter, per diem, eight dollars.

Sergeant-at-Arms, per diem, five dollars.

Translator for Congress, per diem, five dollars.

Door Keeper, per diem, five dollars.

SEC. 2. *Be it further enacted*, That the heads of departments be furnished with offices, stationary, fuel, lights, &c., at the expense of government.

SEC. 3. *Be it further enacted*, That no portion of the above salaries, or pay of members of congress, shall be allowed except in equal ratio with the payments made the officers and soldiers of the army and navy. *Provided*, however, that this section shall not extend to the reporters and clerks of either house of congress, or to the clerks of any of the departments of the government, or the translator and interpreter, the sergeant-at-arms, and the door keepers of either house of congress.

SEC. 4. *And be it further enacted*, That all secretaries of legation be excluded from the operation of the third section of this act.

IRA INGRAM,
Speaker of the house of representatives.

RICHARD ELLIS,
President pro. tem. of the senate.

Approved Dec. 9, 1836.

SAM. HOUSTON.

AN ACT

Relinquishing one league and labor of Land to Michael B. Menard and others, on the east end of Galveston Island.

SEC. 1. *Be it enacted by the senate and house of representatives of the republic of Texas, in congress assembled*, That all the right, title, and claim which the government of Texas has to one league and one labor of land, lying and situate on, and including the east end of Galveston Island, be, and the same is hereby relinquished, in favor of Michael B. Menard, and such associates as he may hereafter include, and all the right, title, and interest which the government of Texas now has in, and to said land, is hereby vested in the said Michael B. Menard, and such associates as he may hereafter include: *Provided*, that nothing herein contained shall affect the vested rights of third persons.

SEC. 2. *Be it further enacted*, That the president shall issue to the said Michael B. Menard, and such associates as he may include, a quitclaim title to said land, in the name of the republic of Texas.

SEC. 3. *Be it further enacted*, That no quitclaim title shall be issued by the president, until the receipt of some authorized agent of Texas shall be deposited in the office of the secretary of the treasury, acknowledging the receipt, from the said Michael B. Menard, of fifty thousand dollars in cash, or approved acceptances in New Orleans.

SEC. 4. *Be it further enacted*, That should the said Menard not pay, or cause to be paid, to some authorized agent of Texas in New Orleans or Mobile, the sum of thirty thousand dollars in cash, or approved acceptances, by the first day of February next, in the city of New Orleans, then and in that case, this act shall be considered a dead letter, and no such right or title shall vest in the said Menard or his associates, except at the option of the government, which shall be manifested by the acceptance or rejection of said thirty thousand dollars, as aforesaid, after that time; and a special pledge is retained on the property for the faithful payment of the further sum of twenty thousand dollars, and which if not paid within two months after the first payment of thirty thousand dollars, the government shall have the right to pay back the thirty thousand dollars, and declare this act a dead letter.

SEC. 5. *Be it further enacted,* That the government of Texas reserves to itself, all that tract of land from the extreme east end of the Island of Galveston running west on the north side of the Island until it strikes a Bayou a short distance above the present fort, thence up said Bayou to its source, thence in a straight line across the Island to the Gulf, containing fifteen acres more or less; also one block of lots in a suitable part of the town for a Custom House and other public uses, to be selected by an agent to be appointed by the president for that purpose; to be selected on or before the first day of public sale of lots at that place.

SEC. 6. *Be it further enacted,* That if the said M. B. Menard and his associates should fail to comply with the requisitions of this act, they shall forfeit and pay to the government of Texas ten thousand dollars, recoverable in any court having cognizance over the same.

SEC. 7. *And be it further enacted,* That David White of the city of Mobile be, and is hereby appointed a special agent to carry into effect the provisions contained in the fourth section of this act.

IRA INGRAM,
Speaker of the house of representatives.
RICHARD ELLIS,
President pro tem. of the Senate.

Approved Dec. 9, 1836.

SAM. HOUSTON.

AN ACT

Adopting a National Seal and Standard for the Republic of Texas.

SEC. 1. *Be it enacted by the senate and house of representatives of the republic of Texas, in congress assembled,* That for the future the national seal of this republic shall consist of a single star, with the letters "Republic of Texas," circular on said seal, which said seal shall also be circular.

SEC. 2. *Be it further enacted,* That for the future there shall be a national flag, to be denominated the "National Standard of Texas," the conformation of which shall be an azure ground, with a large golden star central.

SEC. 3. *Be it further enacted*, That the national flag for the naval service for the Republic of Texas as adopted by the president at Harrisburg on the ninth day of April, eighteen hundred and thirty-six, the conformation of which is union blue, star central, thirteen stripes prolonged, alternate red and white, be, and the same is hereby ratified and confirmed, and adopted as the future national flag for the naval service for the Republic of Texas.

SEC. 4. *And be it further enacted*, That this act shall take effect and be in force from and after its passage.

IRA INGRAM,
Speaker of the house of representatives.
RICHARD ELLIS,
President pro tem. of the Senate.

Approved Dec. 10, 1836.

SAM. HOUSTON.

AN ACT

Establishing an Agency in the city of Mobile.

SEC. 1. *Be it enacted by the senate and house of representatives of the republic of Texas, in congress assembled*, That from and after the passage of this act, that there shall be, and is hereby established, an agency in the city of Mobile, in the state of Alabama, United States of America.

SEC. 2. *Be it further enacted*, That David White, of the city of Mobile, is hereby made the agent of the government of Texas. The said agent be and is hereby fully authorized to dispose of land scrip, at not less than fifty cents per acre; the proceeds of which shall be applied exclusively to the benefit of this government.

SEC. 3. *Be it further enacted*, That the president of this republic be, and is hereby required to deliver over to the said agent, scrip to the amount of one hundred thousand dollars, in due form; and the said agent shall be responsible to this government for the net proceeds of the sale of all scrip which he may receive; and it shall be his duty to report monthly to the president of this republic, all his transactions in any manner touching his agency.

SEC. 4. *Be it further enacted*, That the said agent shall receive, as a compensation for his services, five per cent, on all monies received, and disbursements two and one half per cent.

SEC. 5. *And be it further enacted*, That if, in the opinion of the president of this republic, our commissioners should succeed in making a negotiation, or negotiations to a sufficient amount of money to defray the expenditures of this government, then, and in that case, the president of this republic is authorized and required forthwith to stop the sale of said scrip by said agent.

IRA INGRAM,
Speaker of the house of representatives.

RICHARD ELLIS,
President pro tem. of the Senate.

Approved Dec. 10, 1836.

SAM. HOUSTON.

———

AN ACT

Defining the pay of Mounted Riflemen, now and hereafter in the ranging service on the Frontier.

SEC. 1. *Be it enacted by the senate and house of representatives of the republic of Texas, in congress assembled*, That each and every mounted rifleman, who has entered the ranging service, and not otherwise provided for, be, and is hereby entitled to twenty-five dollars per month as pay, and the same bounty of land as other volunteers in the field.

SEC. 2. *Be it further enacted*, That the pay of officers in the above service shall be as follows: a captain shall be entitled to receive seventy-five dollars per month, a first lieutenant shall receive sixty dollars per month, a second lieutenant, fifty dollars per month, and the orderly sergeant, forty dollars per month; the said officers shall also be entitled to the same bounties of land as officers of the same grade and rank in the volunteer army.

SEC. 3. *And be it further enacted*, That all officers and soldiers, who have been actually engaged in the ranging service since July 1835, shall be included in this act, and shall receive pay for the time he is in service.

IRA INGRAM,
Speaker of the house of representatives.
RICHARD ELLIS,
President pro tem. of the senate.
Approved Dec. 10, 1836.
SAM. HOUSTON.

JOINT RESOLUTION
For the relief of certain Persons.

Resolved, by the senate and house of representatives of the republic of Texas, in congress assembled, That the president be authorized and required to take such measures as in his judgment will effect the release or redemption of our unfortunate prisoners, captured by and in the possession of hostile Indians, said to be on the waters of Red River, either by calling for and sending volunteers against said Indians, or by purchase, treaty, or otherwise.

IRA INGRAM,
Speaker of the house of representatives.
RICHARD ELLIS,
President pro tem. of the senate.
Approved Dec. 10, 1836.
SAM. HOUSTON.

JOINT RESOLUTION
For the relief of Messrs. McKinney and Williams.

SEC. 1. *Resolved, by the senate and house of representatives of the republic of Texas, in congress assembled,* That the president be, and he is hereby authorized and required to appoint a commissioner for the purpose contemplated in the 10th article of the charter of the Bank of Agriculture and Commerce, granted to Samuel M. Williams, by the legislature of the state of Coahuila and Texas, in April, 1835, in order that the parties may exercise and enjoy their privileges under said act.

SEC. 2. *Be it further resolved*, That the secretary of the treasury be, and he is hereby authorized and empowered to negotiate a loan from any bank or banks that may be established in this republic, of sufficient amount for the payment of all just claims held by Messrs. McKinney and Williams against this government; and that should the secretary succeed in negotiating said loan, then he shall give notice to Messrs. McKinney and Williams, to produce their accounts properly authenticated for settlement; and if, on inspection, said accounts be properly authenticated, then the secretary of the treasury shall forthwith proceed to discharge said account: *provided*, that if the secretary of the treasury should effect such loan, that he stipulate in the face of the bond or bonds which he may execute to said bank, on this government, that the notes of said bank shall be recoverable in discharge of said bond or bonds.

IRA INGRAM,
Speaker of the house of representatives.
RICHARD ELLIS,
President pro tem. of the senate.
Approved Dec. 10, 1836.
SAM. HOUSTON.

JOINT RESOLUTIONS,
Authorizing the President to negotiate a Loan for twenty thousand dollars.

SEC. 1. *Resolved, by the senate and house of representatives of the republic of Texas, in congress assembled.* That the president be, and he is hereby authorized and empowered to borrow twenty thousand dollars, for the purpose of purchasing ammunition and munitions of war; and that he be authorized to stipulate for such an amount of interest, payable at such time, as he may be best able to contract for; and that the principal shall be redeemed at such time as may be agreed on.

SEC. 2. *Be it further resolved*, That the president is hereby authorized to sell sufficient land scrip to raise the said sum of twenty thousand dollars, *provided*, that in procuring said twenty thousand dollars, no lands shall be sold for less than fifty cents per acre.

SEC. 3. *And be it further resolved*, That all islands belonging to this republic shall be, and are hereby reserved for the government use, except the president be authorized specially by congress to sell them.

IRA INGRAM,
Speaker of the house of representatives.

RICHARD ELLIS,
President pro tem. of the senate.

Approved Dec. 10, 1836.

SAM. HOUSTON.

JOINT RESOLUTIONS,

Authorizing the President to issue Scrip to the amount of five hundred thousand Acres of Land.

SEC. 1. *Resolved, by the senate and house of representatives of the republic of Texas, in congress assembled*, That the president be, and he is hereby authorized and required to sign land scrip to the amount of five hundred thousand acres, and transmit the same to Thomas Toby of New Orleans, for the purpose of being sold: *provided*, that said scrip shall not be sold for a less sum than fifty cents an acre: *and further provided*, that should the bonds of this government, to the amount of five hundred thousand dollars, be previously sold, then, and in that case it shall be the duty of the president to recall said scrip, and forbid the further selling of the same.

SEC. 2. *And be it further resolved*, That the said Toby, with the proceeds arising from the sale of said scrip be, and is hereby authorized and required to fulfill all legal obligations into which he may have entered as agent of this government, on the faith of the authority given him by the president "ad interim," for the selling of land scrip; and that he be authorized and required to pay all legal debts contracted on the faith of the same.

IRA INGRAM,
Speaker of the house of representatives.

RICHARD ELLIS,
President pro tem. of the senate.

Approved Dec. 10, 1836.

SAM. HOUSTON.

JOINT RESOLUTION,

Defining the duties of the heads of the departments of government.

Be it resolved by the senate and house of representatives of the republic of Texas, in congress assembled, That it shall be, and is hereby made the duty of the heads of departments, composing the president's cabinet, to wit: the secretaries of state, of war, of the navy, of the treasury, and of the attorney general of the republic, to reside permanently at the seat of government of the same, unless absent on leave of the president, and in conformity with the constitution and the laws; to conform to and execute the instructions of the president, whether general or particular; and to give respectively and collectively, such needful aid and counsel whenever required so to do by the chief magistrate of the republic, as may be requisite to a firm, wholesome and harmonious administration of the government.

IRA INGRAM,
Speaker of the house of representatives.

RICHARD ELLIS,
President pro tem. of the senate.

Approved Dec. 13, 1836.

SAM. HOUSTON.

––––––––

AN ACT,

For the relief of Mrs. Mary Millsaps.

SEC. 1. *Be it enacted by the senate and house of representatives of the republic of Texas, in congress assembled,* That any of the quartermasters or commissaries to whom Mrs. Mary Millsaps may apply, shall be, and are hereby authorized to furnish said Mary Millsaps and family with all the provisions and clothing necessary to their comfort; and if the quartermasters or commissaries to whom said Mary Millsaps shall apply, have not such necessaries in possession, he or they shall be, and is hereby authorized to purchase them on the account of the government, and render an account of the same to the secretary of the treasury.

IRA INGRAM,
Speaker of the house of representatives.

RICHARD ELLIS,
President pro tem. of the senate.

Approved Dec. 13, 1836.

SAM. HOUSTON.

————

AN ACT,
Locating temporarily the seat of government.

SEC. 1. *Be it enacted by the senate and house of representatives of the republic of Texas, in congress assembled*, That from and after the first day of April next, the seat of government for the republic of Texas shall be established at the town of Houston, on Buffalo Bayou, until the end of the session of congress which shall assemble in the year one thousand eight hundred and forty.

SEC. 2. *Be it further enacted*, That the president be, and he is hereby authorized to cause to be erected a building suitable for the temporary accommodation of the congress of the republic, and such other buildings as may be necessary for the accommodation of the different departments of the government, at the said seat of government: *provided*, the sum or sums so expended shall not exceed fifteen thousand dollars.

SEC. 3. *And be it further enacted*, That the seat of government as aforesaid, shall be located during the present session of congress, by joint vote of both houses.

IRA INGRAM,
Speaker of the house of representatives.

RICHARD ELLIS,
President of the senate pro tem.

Approved Dec. 15, 1836.

SAM. HOUSTON.

LAWS

AN ACT,

To establish and organize the Supreme Court, and to define the powers and jurisdiction thereof.

SEC. 1. *Be it enacted by the senate and house of representatives of the republic of Texas, in congress assembled*, That there shall be established in this republic a court, to be styled the Supreme Court of the Republic of Texas, which court shall consist of one supreme judge, to be styled the Chief Justice; to be elected by joint vote of both houses of congress, and such judges as shall be elected judges of the district courts, who shall continue in office during the time prescribed by the constitution. The chief justice shall receive a salary of five thousand dollars per annum, payable semi-annually at the treasury of the republic.

SEC. 2. The supreme court shall be held annually at the seat of government, on the first Monday in December, and a majority of all the judges shall be necessary to constitute such court.

SEC. 3. The said supreme court shall have jurisdiction over, and shall hear and determine all manner of pleas, plaints, motions, causes, and controversies, civil and criminal, which may be brought before it from any court in this republic, either by appeal or other legal process, and which shall be cognizable in said supreme court according to the constitution and laws of this republic: *provided*, that no appeal shall be granted, nor shall any cause be removed into the supreme court in any manner whatever until after final judgment or decree in the court below, except in cases particularly provided for by law.

SEC. 4. When by appeal, or in any other manner permitted by law, the judgment, sentence or decree of the court below shall be reversed, the supreme court shall proceed to render such judgment, or pronounce such sentence or decree as the court below should have rendered or pronounced, except it be necessary, in consequence of the decision of the supreme court, that some matter of fact be ascertained, or damages be assessed by a jury, or when the matter to be decreed is uncertain, in either of which cases the suit, action, or prosecution, as the case may be, shall be remanded to the court from which it was brought for a more definite decision.

SEC. 5. When a final judgment or decree shall be rendered or pronounced in any cause brought before the supreme court by appeal or otherwise, it shall be the duty of the clerk of said court to certify the final judgment or decree to the clerk of the court from which such cause was brought, within twenty days after the adjournment of the supreme court at which such final judgment or decree was rendered or pronounced, together with a bill of all costs which shall have accrued, and damages, if any assessed in the said supreme court, and it shall be the duty of every clerk of the court from which such cause was removed, on receiving such certificate, to issue executions on such final judgment for the purpose of having it carried into effect, in the same manner as though it had been rendered in the court below.

SEC. 6. The sentence of the supreme court in all criminal prosecutions brought before such court from any other courts, shall be executed in like manner in all respects as if such sentence had been rendered in the court wherein the prosecution originated, and the sheriff of the proper county shall be charged with the execution of such sentence.

SEC. 7. In all cases taken to the supreme court, in case the copy of the record in the cause below shall not be filed with the clerk of the supreme court, on or before the first day of the term to which such case was taken or returnable, it shall be lawful for the court, on motion of the defendant in appeal, and on producing a copy of the citation duly served on the defendant to dismiss the cause, but the same may be reinstated at any time during the term, if good cause be shown to the satisfaction of the court why a copy of the record was not filed in due time.

SEC. 8. The said court, or any judge thereof, in vacation, may grant writs of injunction, supersedeas, and such other writs as the laws permit to the judgments or decrees of the county or district courts, on such terms and conditions as the laws may prescribe in cases of appeals, and also to grant writs of habeas corpus, and all other remedial writs and process granted by said judges, by virtue of their office, agreeably to the principles and usages of law, returnable as the law directs, either to the supreme court or before any judge of said court, as the nature of the case may require.

SEC. 9. In all cases of appeal to the supreme court the trial shall be on the facts as found by the jury in the court below; and if the facts should not be stated in a manner sufficiently full and clear to enable the supreme court to give its judgment, then and in that case the said court shall remand the said cause to the proper court for a new trial, in order that the facts may be fully and clearly established, and this act shall be construed to extend to appeals taken to the superior courts of Texas, as established by the law of eighteen hundred and thirty-four, which cases remain yet undecided.

SEC. 10. For the said supreme court, one clerk shall be appointed in the following manner: in term time the appointment shall be made by an order entered of record in the proceedings of the court, and the person so appointed, before he enters on the duties of his office, shall take the oath prescribed in the constitution in open court, and shall enter into bond with two securities, to be approved by the court, payable to the president of the republic and his successors in office, in the penalty of twenty thousand dollars, conditioned for the faithful performance of the duties of his office; and that he seasonably record the judgments, decrees, decisions, and orders of the said court, and deliver over to his successor in office all records, minutes, books, papers, and whatever belongs to his said office of clerk, which bond shall be recorded in the clerk's office of said court, and immediately thereafter be deposited in the office of the secretary of state, and shall be void on the first recovery, but may be put in suit and prosecuted by the party injured, until the amount thereof be recovered; in vacation the appointment shall be made by the chief justice, and the person so appointed shall give bond and security, and take the oath as above prescribed, which bond shall be recorded and deposited in the same manner as though the appointment had been made in term time, and may be prosecuted and put in suit in like manner: an authenticated copy, of said bond shall be received in evidence in any court in this republic in the same manner as the original would be if it were present in court.

SEC. 11. The said clerk shall hold his office for the term of four years from his appointment, but may be removed therefrom for neglect of duty or misdemeanor in office, by the supreme court, on motion of which, the clerk against whom complaint is made, shall have ten days previous notice, specifying the particular negligence or misdemeanor in office with which he stands charged, and in every such case the said court shall determine both the law and the fact;

and whenever the necessity occurs, the supreme court may appoint a clerk *pro tempore*.

SEC. 12. The successor in office of any clerk shall receive into his possession, all papers, books, stationary, and every thing belonging to the said office; and should the person or persons having possession of the same, refuse to give them up on demand made, it shall be the duty of the clerk to give information thereof to the attorney general, who shall prosecute such person or persons, in the name of the republic, before any court having jurisdiction of the same, and on conviction the person so offending shall be fined in the sum of ten thousand dollars, for the use of the republic.

SEC. 13. If any clerk of the supreme court shall knowingly make any false entry or change any record in his keeping belonging to his office, every such clerk, so offending, shall, on conviction thereof, be fined and imprisoned at the discretion of the court, and shall also be liable to the action of the party aggrieved.

SEC. 14. The clerk of the said court shall carefully preserve the transcripts of records certified to his court, and all papers relative thereto, docketing all causes brought by appeal or otherwise, in the order he shall receive them, that they may be heard in the same course, unless the court, for good cause shown, direct any to be heard out of its term; and shall faithfully record the decision and proceedings of said court, and certify the same to the proper courts, and all causes shall be tried by the said supreme court at the return term, unless satisfactory cause can be shown for a continuance.

SEC. 15. The clerk of the district court shall receive and pay to the clerk of the supreme court, all costs that may have accrued in the supreme court in any cause or controversy which may have been brought into the supreme court from such district court, wherein a final judgment or decree shall be rendered, and any clerk failing to pay such costs on demand, after he shall have received the same, may be proceeded against by motion in the supreme court in the same manner that sheriffs may be proceeded against for money received on executions.

SEC. 16. A certified copy of the bond required by law to be given by the appellant or plaintiff in the appeal, shall be transmitted by the clerk of the court below, with a transcript of the record of the cause in which such appeal was taken, or which may be taken in any other way to the supreme court; and in case the judgment or decree of the court below shall be affirmed, or the appellant shall fail to prosecute the same to effect, the supreme court shall enter up judgment or decree against all the obligors in such bond, both principal and security for the debt, damages, and costs which may be adjudged to the appellee; and it shall be the duty of the court below, on the certificate of the clerk of the supreme court, to issue executions thereon accordingly.

SEC. 17. In all cases decided by the supreme court, the judgment or decree of the court shall be pronounced publicly, with the reasons of the court for the same.

SEC. 18. All writs and processes issuing from the supreme court shall bear test of the clerk of such court, and shall be under the seal of said court and signed by the clerks thereof, and may be directed to the sheriff or other proper officer of any county in the republic, and shall be by him executed according to the commands thereof, and returned to the court from which they emanated; and whenever such writ or process shall not be executed, the clerk of said court is hereby authorized and required to issue another like writ or process upon the application of the party suing out the former writ or process; and when any person, plaintiff or defendant, in any suit depending in the said court, shall be dead, it shall be lawful for the clerk of the said court, during the recess of the court, upon application, to issue proper process, to enable the court to proceed to a final judgment or decree in the names of the representatives of such deceased person.

SEC. 19. The said court may adjourn from day to day, or for such longer period as they may think necessary to the ends of justice and the determination of the business before them; and there shall be no discontinuance of any suit, process, matter, or thing returned to or depending in the supreme court, although sufficient number of judges shall not attend at the commencement, or any other day of the term; but if a sufficient number shall fail to attend at the commencement of any term, or at any time during the term, any judge of the said court, or the sheriff attending the same, may adjourn the said court from day to day for six days successively; at which time, if a majority of the judges do not attend, it shall be the duty of the judge or sheriff to adjourn the court to term in course.

SEC. 20. No judge of the supreme court shall sit in any cause wherein he is directly or indirectly interested, or if he shall have been of counsel for either party in such cause; but although one or more of the judges of the supreme court be interested in the event of any suit, matter, or thing, depending therein, the same shall be finally decided by the other judges, if there be a number of judges not so interested sufficient to constitute a court; and in case a majority of said judges shall be interested in any cause depending in said court or of any kind to either party within the third degree, it shall be the duty of the congress to appoint, by joint resolution, one or more persons learned in the law to supply the places of the judges so interested, who shall hear and determine all such causes.

SEC. 21. Whenever the supreme court shall be equally divided in opinion, on hearing any appeal or other matter, the judgment or decree of the court below shall be affirmed.

SEC. 22. The sheriff of the county in which the supreme court shall be held, shall be the sheriff of said court, and shall attend the same with a sufficient number of deputies accordingly: and the sheriff and his deputies shall be bound to perform the duties of such.

SEC. 23. The supreme court shall have power to punish any person for a contempt of such court: *provided* such punishment shall not exceed, for each contempt, a fine of one hundred dollars, and imprisonment for six days.

SEC. 24. The chief justice shall cause to be procured a seal for the use of the supreme court, with the style of the Supreme Court around the margin in circular form, with a star of five points in the centre.

SEC. 25. The chief justice and the district judges shall be sworn into office by any one of the primary judges heretofore appointed by law.

SEC. 26. *And be it further enacted*, That the supreme court shall have power from time to time to establish rules of proceeding for the government of said courts, and in the several district courts in this republic: *provided* such rules be not inconsistent with the constitution and laws of the republic.

IRA INGRAM,
Speaker of the house of representatives.

RICHARD ELLIS,
President of the senate pro tem.

Approved Dec. 15, 1836.

SAM. HOUSTON.

JOINT RESOLUTIONS,

For the relief of G. & T. H. Borden.

SEC. 1. *Be it resolved, by the senate and house of representatives of the republic of Texas, in congress assembled,* That the president be, and he is hereby authorized to issue an order on David White, for the sum of two thousand two hundred and thirty-eight dollars twenty-seven cents, in favor of G. & T. H. Borden; and that such order, bearing legal interest, be received as cash, and paid by David White, as agent of Texas, out of any money he may have or receive for the republic of Texas.

SEC. 2. *And be it further resolved,* That the full amount of a contract between the Messrs. G. & T. H. Borden, on the one part, and a joint committee of both houses on the other, the date of the first payment terminating on the eleventh instant, and amounting to two thousand six hundred and sixty-two dollars fifty-six cents, be liquidated in the manner aforesaid.

IRA INGRAM,
Speaker of the house of representatives.

RICHARD ELLIS,
President pro tem. of the senate.

Approved Dec. 15, 1836.

SAM. HOUSTON.

––––––

AN ACT,

Making appropriations for paying the expenses of the government of Texas.

SEC. 1. *Be it enacted by the senate and house of representatives of the republic of Texas, in congress assembled*, That there is hereby appropriated, out of any money in the treasury not otherwise appropriated, the following sums of money, for defraying the expenses of the government, in part, for the years 1836 and 1837, to wit: For defraying the expenses of the navy, one hundred and fifty thousand dollars; for the expenses of the army, seven hundred thousand dollars; for the executive and civil departments of the government, one hundred and fifty thousand dollars, making an appropriation of one million of dollars; which said one million of dollars, the secretary of the treasury is hereby authorized and required to pay out of the treasury, out of any money therein, not otherwise appropriated by law.

SEC. 2. *And be it further enacted*, That if there should be no monies in the treasury when the same may be demanded according to law, of the secretary of the treasury, then and in that case he shall issue scrip to the person or persons lawfully entitled to the same.

IRA INGRAM,
Speaker of the house of representatives.

RICHARD ELLIS,
President pro tem. of the senate.

Approved Dec. 15, 1836.

SAM. HOUSTON.

AN ACT,

Establishing regulations and instructions for the government of the naval service of Texas.

OFFICERS IN GENERAL.

ART. 1. Every officer is to repair to the squadron or vessel to which he shall be appointed, without delay after receiving orders.

ART. 2. Every officer, from the time of his joining the squadron or vessel to which he shall be appointed, to the time of his removal, is to be constant in his attention to his duty; never absenting himself, except on public service, without the consent of his commander, nor shall he remain out of the vessel during the night, nor after the setting of the watch, without having obtained express permission to that effect.

ART. 3. Every officer is directed to wear his uniform at all times while on public service, and it will be the duty of commanders and others to prevent any change whatever from being made in that which now is, or hereafter may be established for the navy.

ART. 4. Every officer is to conduct himself with proper respect to his superiors, and to show every respect and attention to those under his orders, having a due regard to their situation, and invariably to deport himself in every situation so as to be an example of morality, regularity, and good order, to all persons attached to the naval service. He will observe attentively the conduct of all under his command, encouraging and commending the meritorious, and censuring, punishing, or reporting to his superiors the misconduct of those who may deserve it.

ART. 5. If an inferior shall be oppressed by his superior, or observe any misconduct in him, he is not to fail in his respect towards him, but he is to represent such oppression or misconduct to the captain of the vessel, or to the commander of the squadron in which he serves, or to the secretary of the navy in writing.

ART. 6. Every officer is strictly enjoined to avoid all unnecessary expenditure of money or stores belonging to the public, and as far as may depend on him, to prevent the same in others.

ART. 7. Every officer is strictly enjoined to report to his commander, or to the secretary of the navy, as circumstances may require, any neglect, collusion, or fraud discovered by him, in contractors, agents, or other persons employed in the supplying of vessels with provisions or stores, or in executing any work in the naval department, either on board vessel or on shore, whether or not such provisions or stores are under his own charge, or such work under his own inspection, or that of any other officer. But in making such representations he will be held accountable for all vexatious and groundless charges exhibited by him in manner aforesaid.

ART. 8. Every officer is strictly forbidden to have any concern or interest in the purchasing of, or contracting for supplies of provisions or stores of any kind for the navy, or in any works for or appertaining to it; neither shall he receive any emolument or gratuity of any kind, either directly or indirectly, on account of such purchases, contracts, or works, from any person or persons whatever.

ART. 9. Every commander, before he leaves his command, is to sign all books, accounts, and certificates, which may be necessary to enable officers to pass their respective accounts, or to receive their pay: *provided* he be satisfied that such books, accounts, and certificates, are correct, as by the assurance of the purser, who will be held accountable for all errors and improprieties appearing in papers bearing his signature.

ART. 10. If any officer shall receive an order from his superior, contrary to the general instructions of the secretary of the navy, or to any particular order he may have received from the said secretary of the navy, or any other superior, from whom he shall have received said orders; and if, after such representation, the superior shall still insist upon the execution of his order, the officer is to obey him, and report the circumstance to the commander of the vessel, to the commander of the squadron, or the secretary of the navy, as may be proper.

ART. 11. The pay of every officer shall be held answerable for any loss, embezzlement, or damage occurring through neglect of the public stores, and for all unnecessary expense.

COMMANDER-IN-CHIEF.

ART. 1. Every officer appointed to the command of a squadron, shall obtain the most correct information of the state, qualities, and number of the vessels and crews under his command; the order and discipline observed in them; the quantity and quality of provisions and stores on hand, and their fitness for the service intended. He shall acquaint himself also with the skill, capacity, and information of the commanders and other officers, that he may be enabled to select for particular services, those best qualified by their peculiar abilities and sound knowledge to perform them. He shall use every exertion to equip expeditiously the squadron, and report to the secretary of the navy any defects he may discover in the vessels or their supplies, which may unfit them for the service intended.

ART. 2. He shall keep the squadron in the most perfect condition for service that circumstances will admit of, and make their repairs as far as may be in his power, by the artificers and others belonging to the vessel under his command.

ART. 3. He shall take every favorable opportunity to exercise the vessels under his command, in performing all such evolutions as may be necessary in the presence of an enemy; and on all occasions he is to be careful that a proper example of alertness and attention is shown to the squadron by the vessel which carries his flag.

ART. 4. He shall be attentive in battle to the conduct of every vessel or officer under his command, in order that he may be enabled to correct their errors, and prevent any bad effects from misconduct, and to make a true statement, to the end that they may be rewarded or punished as their conduct may really deserve.

ART. 5. He shall direct the crews of the respective vessels under his command to be frequently mustered, and cause inquiries to be made into the qualities of the men, and their fitness for the stations in which they may be rated.

ART. 6. He shall inspect into the state of every vessel under his command, and the order, discipline and attention to cleanliness, and the modes adopted for the preservation of health, and the degree of attention paid to the regulations and instructions of the navy.

ART. 7. He shall not order any commander to take on board passengers, or to have supernumeraries, unless there should be strong reasons for so doing; and in such case he shall state his reasons in his order for that purpose.

ART. 8. He shall inform the secretary of the navy of all his proceedings relative to the service upon which he may be employed.

ART. 9. He shall correspond regularly with the secretary of the navy, informing him of all orders given by him, relating to the duties respectively connected with his command; and it shall be his duty to point out such naval improvements as his observation may enable him to suggest, and such defects and neglects as may come under his notice.

ART. 10. When it shall become absolutely necessary to suspend from employment, an officer having charge of stores, he may appoint another to act in his stead, until the pleasure of the secretary of the navy be known. He shall report by the first opportunity, an account of the circumstances which may have caused the suspension, and order a survey to be held, and an inventory of stores to be taken; one copy of which he shall forward to the navy department, and another he shall deliver to the officer taking charge of the stores, who will open accounts of the receipts, returns, conversions, and issues, from the period of closing the survey.

ART. 11. He may in like manner, and for good reason, suspend from their stations, the captains or other officers under his command, and on a foreign station appoint others to act in their places, until the pleasure of the secretary of the navy be known; but in these cases he shall immediately transmit an account thereof to the secretary of the navy, specifying his reasons for so doing, and furnish the captain or other officers with a duplicate of the same.

ART. 12. He shall not, without good and sufficient reason, to be immediately communicated to the secretary of the navy, alter the appointments assigned to officers at the period of fitting out.

ART. 13. He shall preserve the instructions and orders received by him, and all other papers and correspondence relating to the service upon which he may be ordered in the most intelligible form, and at the end of every cruise he shall send to the secretary of the navy a narrative of his proceedings, accompanied by a fair copy of such official correspondence as may have any connection with the facts therein stated.

ART. 14. He shall conform to the standing rules of the navy in such directions as he shall give to established agents, and incur no expense that the public service does not render absolutely necessary.

ART. 15. He shall have no private interest in the procurement of stores or provisions for the public service, nor in any way interfere with the purchase or procurement of them, where there are proper officers for that purpose, except when an absolute necessity arises for his making use of his credit or authority to obtain them.

ART. 16. He shall obey all orders received from the secretary of the navy, and exact a strict attention to them from all persons under his command.

ART. 17. In the purchase of provisions or stores at places where no regular agent is established, he may appoint one for the purpose of obtaining the necessary supply, and he may himself contract for the whole quantity required, or direct each captain to purchase what the vessel under his command may require; but in either case the amount of the bills drawn will be charged to his account, until satisfactory vouchers are received to show that the articles were of a suitable quality, and purchased at the lowest rate.

ART. 18. He shall, as far as may be practicable, when no regular agents may be established, have the public works which it may be necessary to have done, on contract, executed at the lowest rates, and on the most reasonable terms, giving public notice, that tenders may be received from those disposed to contract: copies of which contracts shall be sent by him to the secretary of the navy.

ART. 19. No boats or vessels shall be hired for the use of the squadron, without the consent of the commander, and he will be careful that such consent is not given, except when the service required cannot be performed by the boats of the vessel under his command.

ART. 20. Foreign agents are to be paid by bills drawn on the secretary of the navy, at the regular rates of exchange, unless otherwise instructed by the secretary of the navy; or bills may be disposed of, and the proceeds applied towards reimbursing them; but in either case the certificates of three respectable merchants, and the approval of the commander of the squadron, must be forwarded with the letter of advice. These bills shall in all cases be drawn by the pursers of the respective vessels for the amount of the provisions or stores received, and approved by the commander of the squadron, or by the captain of the vessel when acting separately.

ART. 21. The commander of a squadron shall direct frequent examinations to be made into the hospital establishments, and sick quarters under his command, and cause every attention to be paid to the comforts of the sick. He shall cause the examining officers to make him a written report of their state and condition.

ART. 22. Should the commander of a squadron be killed or disabled in battle, his flag shall continue flying while the enemy remains in sight, and the officer next in command shall be informed thereof, and take command of the squadron.

ART. 23. On the death of the commander of a squadron, the officer who succeeds him shall enjoy all the pay and emoluments of commander, in the same manner as his predecessor, until the pleasure of the secretary of the navy be known, but he is not to assume any badge of distinction, or hoist any flag which his rank does not entitle him to.

ART. 24. The commander of a squadron shall not resign his command or quit his station, unless the bad state of his health shall render a change of climate or situation absolutely necessary: and in such case he shall not weaken the squadron by taking from it a vessel, the service of which may be necessary.

ART. 25. When the commander of a squadron shall resign his command, he shall deliver to his successor the originals of all secret instructions, orders and signals, and authenticated copies of all other unexecuted instructions and orders, together with such information as may be in his possession relative to the service to be performed.

ART. 26. In the absence of the commander of the squadron, the senior officer shall be governed by the foregoing instructions, and shall superintend the various duties to be performed; for the due execution of which he will be held responsible.

OF STORES AND PROVISIONS.

THE CAPTAIN.

ART. 1. The signature of the captain shall be affixed to all papers having reference to the expenses of the vessel.

ART. 2. On taking command, he shall demand of his predecessor an inventory of all the articles which are on board, and if he command the vessel until she is paid off, he shall send such inventory with his accounts to the auditor of the treasury.

ART. 3. He shall cause a careful examination to be made of all articles received on board for the use of the vessel, and if he fail to do so he will be alone accountable for any evils resulting from defect or deficiencies in them: *provided* such defect or deficiencies were passed over at the receipt of the articles from want of due examination thereof.

ART. 4. When the duties of the ship will admit of it, he shall permit the purser to use the boats for the purpose of conveying on board provisions, stores, and other necessaries for the use of the vessel.

ART. 5. He shall not permit his stores to be applied to private uses, wasted, or, without absolute necessity, converted to other purposes than those for which they were intended; and whenever he shall think it necessary to order any extraordinary expenditure or conversion of stores or provisions, his order for that purpose shall be given in writing, stating the reason or reasons for such extraordinary expenditure or conversion, which order shall be preserved and produced by the officer having charge of the stores so expended or converted, at the settlement of his accounts.

ART. 6. If any stores or provisions shall be lost, destroyed or embezzled, the circumstances shall be noted in the log book of the vessel; and if, through neglect or design, they should be totally lost, they shall be charged to the offender, and he be brought to punishment.

ART. 7. He is to use the utmost economy in every thing which relates to the expenses of his vessel and the public service confided to him, using every article for the purpose for which it was originally intended, and making his supplies and means last as long as possible. He is not to use sails for covering boats, nor for awnings, nor to convert canvass into sails not allowed for the service, nor to any other purpose than that for which they were supplied, unless they shall have at first been surveyed and reported unfit for their proper use; nor shall he make any alterations in the vessel under his command without the permission of the commander-in-chief, or that of the secretary of the navy.

ART. 8. He shall examine the weekly returns of expenditures, and, with the master, sign those made monthly; which, when so signed, are to be delivered to the officers having charge of stores, to be presented by them at the settlement of their accounts.

ART. 9. He may grant to private vessels of Texas, and to foreign vessels, when absolutely necessary, such supplies of provisions and stores as they stand in need of; giving the officers having charge of them written orders to that effect, and taking from the master or commander of the vessel so supplied, three receipts, and three bills of exchange, drawn in favor of the secretary of the navy on his owner, or those concerned in the vessel, for the real amount of the articles furnished; which bills, and two of the receipts, shall be transmitted to the secretary of the navy, and the circumstance noted on the accounts and log book of the vessel.

ART. 10. When it becomes necessary to purchase stores, they shall be delivered to the proper officers of the vessel, who shall sign receipts for them, and they are to be charged at their cost by the purser of the vessel, against such officers, in their accounts; and such charge or charges shall be transmitted to the auditor of the treasury, to stand against their pay until accounted for.

ART. 11. On the death of an officer having charge of stores, his public papers shall be separated from those of a private nature, the former to be forwarded by safe conveyance to the auditor of the treasury, and the latter, together with his private effects, to be put in charge of such officer as the captain of the vessel may appoint for that purpose, to be preserved for the benefit of the legal representative of the deceased; unless from particular circumstances, the captain should deem it advisable to dispose of them at public sale; in which case a duplicate of the inventory, with an account of the disposal or sale, shall be transmitted to the auditor of the treasury.

ART. 12. If an officer, having charge of stores, should, from any accidental circumstance, be separated from his vessel, the captain shall proceed to survey and ascertain the state of the stores, as though such officer were actually dead, or discharged; and he shall, as in a like case, appoint another officer to act in his place, giving the earliest intelligence of his proceedings to the auditor of the treasury.

ART. 13. When a ship or vessel cuts, slips, or parts her cable, the captain shall, as soon as circumstances will admit, endeavour to recover the anchor or cable lost; and should it appear that no exertion for that purpose was made by him, the value of the articles will be charged against his pay; if the vessel put to sea without recovering them, the senior officer present shall endeavour to recover them, but no vessels are to be hired for the purpose if the boats and crew of the squadron are able to effect it. If neither of them, however, have an opportunity of recovering them, the captain of the vessel whose cable was thus cut, slipped, or parted, shall, without delay, give an account to the commander-in-chief, or to the navy agent, taking care to state particularly the bearings and distances of the most suitable places to mark the spot where the anchor lies, to the end that means may be immediately adopted for recovering it.

ART. 14. He shall attend with all the officers of his vessel when the crew is paid off, and examine carefully, to discover if any articles are concealed with a view to embezzlement, and report to the secretary of the navy the character of each officer serving under him, particularly as to his sobriety, diligence, activity and abilities.

ART. 15. A captain, when not under the immediate command of a superior, shall be held responsible for all accidents arising from negligence during his absence from the vessel he commands, where his presence might have prevented such accidents, unless he be absent on public duty, or by permission of the secretary of the navy. He shall also be held responsible for all accidents arising from the absence of the officers and crew of the vessel he commands, unless they be absent on public duty, or by permission of the secretary of the navy.

ART. 16. When the vessel goes into port to refit, he is to order a minute and careful survey of all stores, and call upon the proper officers and prepare lists of all such us are damaged as required to be replaced.

ART. 17. He is not to suffer any except the most careful of the officers and men to have berths, or to sleep in the orlop or cable tiers, in which lights are never to be used without his express permission, and them in good lanterns; nor is he to allow any person to smoke tobacco in any part of the vessel except the galley. He is strictly forbid the sticking of candles against the beams, the side or any other part of the vessel; to enjoin it upon the officers never to read in bed by the lights either of lamps or candles, nor to have any lights in their cabins without some person to attend them; to cause the funnel hole to be well secured by lead or otherwise, and the funnels to be cleaned every morning before the fires are lighted; to cause all fires to be extinguished, and lights to be put out, at the setting of the watch by the master-at-arms and ship's corporal, except such as he shall permit to be kept burning; and to give the most positive orders, and most rigidly to enforce them, that no lighted handle be carried into the spirit room on any pretext what- ever, while drawing or pumping of spiritous liquors, which duty shall be performed only by day, except on great emergencies occurring in the night.

ART. 18. He is not to suffer any person whatever to suttle on board, nor to sell any kind of beer, wines, or spiritous liquors on board to the ship's company. He is not to allow the men to sell, exchange, or in any manner dispose of the slop clothes or bedding with which they are supplied, and as far as possible to prevent any traffic amongst them that would induce them to draw from the purser tobacco, sugar, tea, slop clothes, or any other articles in larger quantities than are usually supplied.

ART. 19. He is to be particularly attentive to the comfort and cleanliness of the men, directing them to wash themselves frequent- ly, and to change their linen at least twice every week. He is never to suffer them to sleep in wet clothes or wet beds if it can possibly be avoided; and to cause them frequently, particularly after bad weather, to shake their clothes and bedding in the air, and to expose them to the sun and wind.

ART. 20. As cleanliness, dryness, and pure air essentially con- duce to health, he is to exert his utmost endeavors to ensure these to the ship's company in the most extensive degree. He is to cause the upper decks to be washed every morning, and the lower decks as often as may be necessary when the weather will admit of their being properly aired and dried; to be swept every meal, and the dirt thrown overboard. He is to cause the hammocks to be carried on deck, and the ports to be opened as often as the weather will permit, and no more chests or bags to be kept on the lower gun deck than may be necessary for the comfort of the men; so that as few interruptions as possible may be opposed to a free circulation of air. He is to cause the wind sails and ventilators to be kept in continual operation; the vessel to be pumped out daily.

ART. 21. The clothing issued to the men is to be suitable to the season; but the wearing of flannel shirts is to be encouraged and permitted at all seasons and in all climates.

ART. 22. The practice of detaining boats on shore for officers, after night is set in, is strictly prohibited.

ART. 23. On receiving newly recruited men, the captain will cause an examination into the state of their persons and clothing, and use every measure to guard against the introduction of filth and contagion on board the vessel.

ART. 24. As soon as possible after the ship's company is received on board, he will, with the assistance of the senior lieutenant, master, and boatswain, proceed to examine and rate them according to their abilities, which he is to do without partiality or favor. He is to rate as petty officers those only who shall be found qualified for such stations, and to take especial care that every person in the vessel, without exception, does actually perform the duties of his station in which he is rated. He shall rate none as ordinary seamen who have not been previously at sea twelve months, and are able to go aloft, and perform some of the duties of a seaman; nor shall he rate any as able seamen who have not been previously at sea three years, and are capable of performing most of the duties of a seaman.

ART. 25. He is, without loss of time, to make arrangements for quartering the officers and men, distributing them to the guns, musketry, rigging, &c., to divide them into watches, make out his quarter, station, and watch bills of the names of men stationed at every gun, to muster and exercise them frequently at the great guns, small arms, bending and unbending, loosing, and reefing, and furling sails, sending up and down top gallant-masts and yards, rowing in boats, and every other duty which it may be necessary for seamen to perform at sea and in port.

ART. 26. As occasions may frequently occur on which it may be necessary and of great importance that seamen should be skillful in the use of muskets, the captain is to order a number of sailors to be exercised and trained up to the use of small arms.

ART. 27. No captain shall carry any woman to sea without an order from the secretary of the navy, or from the commander-in-chief of the squadron to which he belongs.

ART. 28. Every captain is required to make himself acquainted with every coast and harbor he may visit, and if practicable, to make charts and drawings of them, provided it can be done without giving offence; all of which he is to forward to the secretary of the navy, accompanied with a journal containing such remarks, description, and information as he may think necessary to give. He is to endeavour to ascertain correctly the latitude and longitude of places little known, the prevalent winds and currents, the soundings, &c., as well as every other information that may be of importance to those who visit the place after him; he will also encourage and offer every facility to such of his officers as are desirous of entering into similar occupations and pursuits; and if any such journals or charts contain observations or remarks which may contribute to the improvement of geography by ascertaining the latitude and longitude, fixing or rectifying the position of places, the height and views of land, charts, plans or descriptions of any port, anchorage ground, coast, island, or dangers little known; remarks relative to the directions and effects of currents, tide or winds, the officers or persons appointed to examine them will make extracts of whatever may appear to merit preservation; and after these extracts have been communicated to the officer or author of the journal from which they have been taken, and that he has certified in writing to the fidelity of his journal, as well as of his charts, plans and views which he has joined to it, the same shall be signed by the officers and examiners, and transmitted with their opinions thereon, to be preserved in the depot of charts, journals, and plans.

ART. 29. Whenever he is to sail from port to port, in time of war, or appearance thereof, he is to give notice to merchant vessels bound his way, and to take them under his care, if they are ready, but not to make unnecessary stay, or deviate from his orders on that account.

ART. 30. He is, by all opportunities, to send an account of his proceedings to the secretary of the navy, and he is to keep up a punctual correspondence with all public officers in whatever concerns them.

ART. 31. He is not to go into any port but such as may be directed by his orders, unless by absolute necessity; and then not to make any unnecessary stay. If employed in cruising, he is to keep the sea, the time required by his orders, or give reasons for acting to the contrary, to the secretary of the navy.

ART. 32. Upon his own removal into another vessel, he is to show the originals of all such orders as have been sent him, and remain unexecuted to his successor, and leave with him attested copies of the same.

ART. 33. He is to leave with his successor a complete muster book, and send all other books and accounts to the officers to whom they respectively relate.

ART. 34. In case of shipwreck, or other disasters whereby the vessel may perish, the officers and men are to stay with the wreck as long as possible, and save all they can.

ART. 35. When any men employed for wages are discharged from one vessel to another, the captain of the vessel from which they may be discharged is immediately to send pay lists of such men to the auditor of the treasury, and the purser of the vessel from which they are so discharged, is also to supply the purser of the ship to which they are transferred, a pay list, stating the balances respectively due them.

ART. 36. He is responsible for the whole conduct and good government of the vessel, and for the due execution of all regulations which concern the several duties of the officers and company of the vessel, who are to obey him in all things which he shall direct for the service of Texas.

ART. 37. The quarter deck must never be left without one commissioned officer at least, and the other necessary officers which the captain may deem proper to attend to the duty of the vessel.

ART. 38. On vessels of Texas being visited by custom house officers, the captain will offer them every facility in the performance of their duties, and if there should be a suspicion of any persons having articles on board, subject to the payment of duties, which such person is desirous of smuggling, he is to give them every possible assistance in discovering such articles, if they are really on board. If he should discover any officer in the act of smuggling or attempting to smuggle, he is immediately to arrest such officer, and report the same to the secretary of the navy, in order that such direction may be given as conduct so injurious to the public, and so disgraceful to an officer shall require.

ART. 39. While in port or roadstead, he is to follow the motions of the senior officer present, by striking or getting up yards and topmasts, loosing or furling sails, and doing any other duties contemporaneously with the vessel which the senior officer commands, unless such senior officer shall dispense with his so doing.

ART. 40. He is to pay every attention to the comforts of the sick and wounded, causing a comfortable place to be provided for them in any part of the vessel where they will be the least incommoded.

ART. 41. He is required to keep copies of all official correspondence.

ART. 42. The captain of a vessel carrying a broad pendant, is on all occasions of duty to consult his commander, and a respect due him requires that he should not inflict any punishment without his knowledge.

ART. 43. If any Texian vessel of war should be wrecked, the captain is to use every possible exertion to save the lives of the crew, and to preserve the stores, provisions, and furniture of the vessel. He is also to endeavour to save the vessel's papers, particularly the muster and slop books, and to take special care to preserve or destroy all signals, secret orders, and instructions, to prevent their falling into improper hands. He is to dispose of the crew in a manner most conducive to their comfort and the public interest, and to be very particular in keeping up a regular and perfect discipline among them, carefully preventing the commission of any irregularity which may give offence to the inhabitants of the country they are in.

ART. 44. He is to lose no time in getting the crew to Texas, to effect which he is authorized to dispose of, on the best terms, the property saved from the wreck, or to draw on the secretary of the navy for the necessary monies.

ART. 45. Whenever any commander of a public vessel of Texas shall find himself placed in such circumstances as shall compel him to strike his flag to an enemy, he is to take especial care to destroy all his secret instructions, signal books, and private signals; and for this purpose they should be always kept fastened to a weight, so heavy as to sink them immediately on being thrown overboard; and on enquiring into the loss of the vessel, he will produce evidence of his having done so.

ART. 46. The vessel and every person on board being placed under the command of the captain, he will be held responsible for every thing done on board. From him will be expected an example of respect and obedience to his superiors, of unremitting attention to his duty, and a cheerful alertness in the execution of it, in all situations, and under all circumstances. He will be expected to observe himself, and strongly to enforce in others, the most rigid economy in the expenditures of public stores; and to show by every means in his power, a steady determination to serve his country with the utmost zeal and fidelity; and although particular duties are hereafter assigned, and various instructions given to every officer in the navy; from him it will be expected that all those, whether officers or others, shall be corrected, or their conduct properly represented, who are disobedient or disrespectful to their superiors, neglectful of their duty, wasteful of public stores, or who by their conduct or conversation shall endeavour to render any officer or other person dissatisfied with his situation or with the service on which he is employed. He is to observe with particular attention the conduct of every officer, and of every other person under his command; that being acquainted with their respective merits, he may assign them such station as they may be qualified to fill; and for arduous and dangerous enterprises may select those whose abilities and courage may afford the best hopes of success. He is to be extremely attentive to every thing done by his clerk, who, being appointed for the sole purpose of assisting him, will be considered as always acting by his order.

ART. 47. The commander of a squadron shall be allowed, on fitting out, to equip his cabin every three years or thereabouts, in lieu of every expense for movable furniture, the sum of five hundred dollars.

ART. 48. There shall be allowed on fitting out to equip the cabin of a captain, every three years or thereabouts, in lieu of every expense for movable furniture, three hundred dollars.

ART. 49. Articles unfit for service must be surveyed by an order from the secretary of the navy, or in the event of a vessel being on a foreign station, by an order from he commander of the station, on the application of the commander of the vessel; and no new articles are to be furnished until the old shall be condemned, which must be certified by the officers holding the survey, and the certificate forwarded to the secretary of the navy.

ART. 50. Articles of cabin furniture broken or lost at sea, shall be replaced by the commander of the vessel at his own expense, unless he shall make it appear by the certificate of two commissioned officers, that such loss or breaking was occasioned by unavoidable casualty, or accidents beyond his control.

OF THE LIEUTENANT.

ART. 1. A lieutenant is to be constantly attentive to his duty, and diligently and punctually to execute all orders for the public service which he may receive from the captain or other senior officer. When he has the watch he is to be constantly on deck, until relieved by the officer who is to succeed him. He is to see that the men are alert and attentive to their duty, that every precaution is taken to prevent accidents from squalls or sudden gusts of wind, and that the vessel is as perfectly prepared for a battle as circumstances shall admit. He is to be particularly careful that the vessel be properly steered, and that a correct account be kept of her way, by the log being duly hove and marked on the log board.

ART. 2. He is to see that the master's mates and midshipmen of the watch are constantly on deck, and attentive to their duty; and he is to order the men of the watch to be frequently mustered, and to report to the captain such as he shall find absent from their duty.

ART. 3. He is to be extremely attentive to keep the vessel in her station in any squadron he may belong to; and he is to inform the captain whenever he apprehends that he shall not he able to do so.

ART. 4. He is to inform the captain of all strange sails that are seen, all signals that are made, all changes of sail made by the commander, all shifting of the wind, and in general of all circumstances which may derange the order in which the squadron is sailing, or prevent the vessel from continuing on the course directed to be steered.

ART. 5. He is to be very particular in delivering to the lieutenant who relieves him on the watch, all orders received by him from the captain or lieutenant he relieved remaining unexecuted; and he is to inform him of all signals made by the commander-in-chief, which still remain to be obeyed. He is to point out to him more especially in the night the situation of the commander-in-chief, and to inform him what sail his vessel was carrying when it could last be ascertained, and whether the vessel was coming up with or dropping astern of him; and he is to give in general whatever other information may be necessary to enable him to keep the vessel on her station, if the squadron be formed in the order of sailing, or to keep well up with it, if it be not so formed.

ART. 6. He is to keep men at the masts' heads during the day, and in proper stations during the night, to look out. He is frequently to remind them of their duty, if necessary, and to relieve them, more or less frequently, according to the state of the weather, and the degree of their attention.

ART. 7. On a strange sail being seen in the night during war, he is to send a midshipman to inform the captain, and is himself to make arrangements for getting the vessel ready for action. He is to keep out of gunshot until every thing is ready, but in doing this he is to be careful not to remove to such a distance as to risk losing sight of her.

ART. 8. He is never to carry so much sail as to endanger the springing of any mast or yard, unless some particular service should require it, and when he does so, he must take care that all the men in the watch are at their stations, ready to shorten sail the moment any increase of wind, or other circumstances shall make it necessary.

ART. 9. In the night he is to take care that the master-at-arms and corporals in their respective watches, are very particular in going the rounds, and that they visit all parts of the vessel every half hour, to see that there is no disturbance among the men, and that no candles or lamps are burning, except such as are expressly allowed.

ART. 10. He is to direct the carpenter to sound the well himself, or direct one of his mates to do it, once at least in every watch, and to see that the ports are well barred; and the gunner or one of his mates to examine once at least in each watch, the state of the lashing of the guns, and to report to him when they have done so.

ART. 11. In the morning he is to direct the boatswain to examine into the state of the rigging, and the carpenter that of the masts and yards; he is to receive their reports, and to inform the captain of any defects they may discover.

ART. 12. He is never to change the course of the vessel without directions from the captain, unless it be necessary to avoid some danger.

ART. 13. If the vessel belongs to, or is in company with any squadron, he is to direct some careful officer to observe the signals made by the commanding officer; but he is never to answer any signal, whether general or addressed particularly to the vessel to which he belongs, unless he is certain that he sees it distinctly, and understands for what purpose it is made; and he is every evening before dark to see that lanterns with candles and every thing necessary for making signals in the night, are ready and in good order; and that the number of guns which may be directed not shotted, are ready for being fired, and to be particularly attentive in preventing any other lights being shown in the vessel when signal lights are hoisted, and when at sea that no light may be seen from the cabin or any part of the vessel.

ART. 14. During a fog he is to be particularly attentive to the guns fired by the commander-in-chief, that by observing any alteration that may take place either in the direction or strength of the report, he may take such steps as may be deemed necessary to prevent the vessel's being separated from the squadron. He is to be very careful to order the drum to be beat, and the bell to be sounded according to the tack the vessel may be on, for the information of vessels that may be near.

ART. 15. He is to see that every occurrence worthy of notice during the watch be properly entered on the log board, and that all signals made in the squadron are correctly minuted, in such a manner as the captain shall direct; and at the end of his watch he is to sign the log board and the report of signals, with the initials of his name; and in like manner, when the occurrences of the day, and the report of the signals have been entered in the log book, he is to sign that with his name at the end of each watch he kept.

ART. 16. He is constantly to ascertain the latitude by observation, at moon, or by double altitude, as circumstances may require, and to keep an account of the vessel's way, specifying the course steered, and the distance run for each twenty-four hours, with the latitude and longitude she is in, and the bearings and distances of some head land from which she sailed, or towards which he may be going, with other particulars, and in any form that the captain shall direct; which account he is to deliver to the captain every day, as soon after noon as the other duties of the vessel will allow.

ART. 17. He is not to make any signal by day or by night, except such as may be necessary to warn vessels of any danger to which they may be exposed, without the direction of the captain.

ART. 18. In time of action, he is to see that all the men under his command are at their quarters, and that they do their duty with spirit and alacrity. He is to be particularly attentive to prevent them from loading the guns improperly; from firing them before they are well pointed, and from wetting them after they have been fired, and he is to be very careful to prevent their making an improper accumulation of powder in any part of his quarters.

ART. 19. He is to be attentive to the conduct of all the ship's company, to prevent all profane swearing and abusive language, all disturbance, noise, and confusion, to enforce a strict obedience to orders, a proper respect to all superiors, and an observance of discipline and good order; and he is to report to the captain all those whose misconduct he shall think deserving of reprehension or punishment.

ART. 20. No boat is to be allowed to come along side, or to go from the vessel, without direction from the lieutenant of the watch. When vessels or boats come along side with provisions, stores, water, &c., he is to see that they are cleared without delay, and that the articles are taken into the vessel with the utmost care, to prevent their suffering any damage; and when any provisions, stores, empty casks, &c., are to be sent from the vessel, he is to be equally attentive in causing them to be put into the vessels or boats appointed to receive them.

ART. 21. In the absence of the captain, the senior lieutenant on board the vessel is to be responsible for every thing done on board; he is to see every part of the duty as punctually performed as if the captain were present.

He may put under arrest any officer whose conduct he shall think so reprehensible as to require it, and he may confine such men as he may think deserving of punishment; but neither he, nor any other lieutenant, who may become commanding officer, is to release an officer from his arrest, nor to release or punish any man who has been confined; for this is to be done by the captain only, unless he be absent from the vessel, with leave from the secretary of the navy, or from his commanding officer, in which case it is to be done only by the senior lieutenant commanding the vessel in the captain's absence.

OF THE MASTER.

ART. 1. A master, when attached to a vessel, is to be constantly attentive to his duty, and diligently and punctually to execute all orders he may receive from the captain or any of the lieutenants of the vessel for the public service.

ART. 2. He is to be present himself at the stowing of the hold, to see that the vessel has the proper quantity of iron or other ballast; and he is to stow her in a manner best qualified to preserve her trim, to make room in the hold, and to admit of the stowage of the water and provisions without risk of damage to the casks. He is to stow away as much wood in the hold as possible; and if it should appear to him that the quantity of wood and coals will not be sufficient for the time for which the vessel is victualled, he is to report it to the captain.

ART. 3. He is to be present when stores and provisions are received on board, to see them carefully and expeditiously hoisted in to prevent their being damaged; and if any of them should appear to him to be in any respect defective, he is to report it to the captain, or the commanding officer on board, that they may be surveyed as soon as the service will admit, and then disposed of in conformity to the report of the survey.

ART. 4. If any provisions are pointed out to him as being older than the rest, he is to stow them in such a way as to admit of their being first hoisted up; and on receiving any subsequent supplies, he is, whenever circumstances will admit, to put the new provisions under the old, that they may be the last expended.

ART. 5. He is to keep the keys of the after hold and spirit room, which, when wanted, he is to deliver to one of the masters mates only, strictly charging him not to suffer a light to be carried into the spirit room; to attend himself, without quitting on any account, the spirit room or after hold while open, to see it properly secured when the service for which it was opened shall be executed, and to return the keys to him as soon as he has done so.

ART. 6. He is to see that the sails are properly fitted with points, robands, earings, &c, ready for being brought to the yards, and that the boatswain has always a sufficient number of spare points, robands, gaskets, mats, plats, knippers, &c., ready for any purpose for which they may be wanted.

ART. 7. He is to be attentive in observing the quantity of every species of provisions hoisted up from the hold, that if the quantity should appear to be more than is necessary for the ship's company, he may inform the captain; he is to attend also to the quantity of wood hoisted up, that he may prevent any improper expenditure of the same.

ART. 8. He is to be particularly careful to prevent any waste or improper expense of water, and never allow of its being started or pumped out in the hold without particular directions from the captain; nor is he to suffer more to be hoisted up in a day than the quantity allowed.

ART. 9. He is every day to report to the captain the quantity of water expended during the last twenty-four hours, and the quantity remaining on board.

ART. 10. He is, with the first lieutenant, to visit the store rooms of the warrant officers, to see that they are kept as clean and as well ventilated as circumstances will admit, that no other than the stores of the vessel are to be put into them, and that the stores are so regulated as to admit of any of them being found when wanted.

ART. 11. He is frequently to inspect the sail room, to see that they are dry, and the rooms in good order. He is to give orders for the repairing of sails immediately on discovering that they require it; and if he should find them or any of the stores at anytime, likely to be damaged by dampness, or by any other cause, he is immediately to represent it to the captain.

ART. 12. He is frequently to examine into the state of the rigging, and to see that the standing rigging is always kept well set up;

to attend himself when it is set up; to examine frequently the running rigging, and to inform the captain when any part of it appears to be no longer serviceable.

ART. 13. At the end of every week he is to examine the boatswain's and the carpenter's accounts of stores expended, and at the end of every month he is, with the first lieutenant, to sign their expense books, which he is to examine with very great attention before he signs them, to prevent the insertion of expenditures which have not been made, or any improper account of those which have.

ART. 14. He is to see that the compasses, the hour and other glasses are properly taken care of, to try them and compare them with each other frequently, to ascertain and prevent the bad effects of any error which may be in them, to see the log-lines and lead-lines correctly marked, and at hand, whenever they may be wanted.

ART. 15. He is, under the command of the captain, to have the charge of navigating the vessel. He is to represent to the captain every possible danger in or near the vessel's course, and the way to avoid it, and if it be immediate, to the lieutenant of the watch; whenever the vessel shall be approaching the land or any shoal, he is to be upon deck, and keep a good lookout, always sounding to inform himself of the situation of the vessel.

ART. 16. He is every day at noon to deliver to the captain, an account of the situation of the vessel, the latitude and longitude she is in, the variation of the compass, the bearings and distance of the place sailed from, or of that to which the vessel is bound, and every other particular which the captain shall direct.

ART. 17. He is to have charge of the ship's log book, which is to be written by the master's mate, under his immediate inspection; he is to compare it every day with the log board, to see that every circumstance which has occurred, is properly catered in it; and he is to send it immediately to the lieutenants, that they may sign their names at the end of their respective watches, while that which happened in them is still fresh in their memories. In the log book he is to enter with very minute exactness each of the following circumstances, viz:

1st – The state of the weather, the directions of the wind, the courses steered, and the distances run, with every occurrence relating to the navigation of the vessel, the setting and the velocity of the currents, and the result of all astronomical observations made to ascertain the situation of the vessel, the variation of the compass, &c.

2d – The loss of masts, yards, boats, &c., the splitting of sails, the blowing away of flags or colors, and all other accidents, with the quantity of each article lost or saved.

3d – Every circumstance relating to the supply, receipts, loss, survey, and returns of slop clothes, provisions, casks, and water; specifying from whom they were received, and to whom they were supplied or returned, and by whose order, if any order were given, with the number of casks and packages written in words at length.

4th – An account of the quantity of every species of stores, purchased for the vessel, or received from, or supplied to any other Texian vessel, or to merchant vessels, or to any foreign vessels or arsenal.

5th – Every alteration made in the allowance of provisions, specifying by whose order such allowance was made.

6th – The marks and numbers of every cask of provisions or bale of slops opened for the use of the vessel's crew, with the quantity it is said to have contained, and the difference, if there is any.

7th – An account of the number of men employed on board who are to be paid for the services they perform, whether hired for that purpose, or lent from other vessels, mentioning the day on which they began, and on which they ceased working, and the number mustered every day. Every entry of the receipt, expenditure, loss, &c., of stores or provisions, is to be carefully examined by the officer who has the charge of them, who is to signify that the account is correct, by signing his name at the bottom of it. After the log book has been signed by the lieutenant, no alteration, however trifling, is to be made in it, without the approbation of the captain, and the perfect recollection of the lieutenant of the watch that such alteration is proper.

ART. 18. At the end of every six calendar months, he is to deliver a copy of the log book for those six months, signed by himself, to the captain, to be transmitted by the first safe opportunity to the secretary of the navy; and at the end of every twelve months he is to deliver the original log book, signed by himself, to the captain, to be kept by him till the vessel is paid off, and then to be sent to the secretary of the navy. If the master be superseded he is to sign the original log book, then in his possession, and to deliver it to his successor, who is to give him a receipt for it.

PURSER.

ART. 1. The purser being the officer appointed to receive and distribute the victualing stores and slops of the vessel, having entered into bonds to the government of Texas, as prescribed by law, is to abide by the following regulations and instructions; and he is not to expect that any irregularity in, or omission of any part thereof, or of the forms referred to therein for keeping his accounts will pass unnoticed.

ART. 2. Every purser attached to a vessel of war shall make to the secretary of the navy a statement of his accounts every six months, and settle his accounts at the treasury every twelve months; nor shall he permit a longer time to elapse without offering his accounts for settlement, if the vessel to which he belongs be in a port, or on the coast of Texas; and in the event of his failing to do so, his pay and emoluments shall cease from the time of the expiration of the twelve months, commencing at the time of his joining the vessel, or at the date of the last settlement.

ART. 3. No purser can be employed or removed from one vessel or station to another, until he shall have settled up his accounts for the vessel or station to which he shall have last belonged, unless specially exempted from doing so by the secretary of the navy.

ART. 4. Before a purser can receive orders to join a vessel or station, or to be removed from one vessel or station to another, he must produce a certificate from the auditor of the treasury, or other satisfactory evidence, that he has settled up his accounts for the last vessel or station to which he belongs, and that the balance against him does not exceed one thousand dollars.

ART. 5. When a purser joins a vessel or station he shall see that it is provided with the necessary articles belonging to his department; take care that the provisions, victualing stores, and slops are of good quality, and demand a survey on those which may appear damaged, or otherwise unfit for the service.

ART. 6. Tobacco will be purchased by the Texian government, and delivered and charged to the purser, at cost and charges; and he will, on the settlement of his accounts, be allowed fifty per cent, on the amount of all tobacco issued; which per centage is to be added to the cost and charges on the article when issued to the crew.

ART. 7. All the slops, clothing, &c., will be charged to the purser, at cost and charges, and he is to be held accountable for the expenditure.

ART. 8. In no case will the purser be credited even for any alleged loss by damage in slops, unless he show, by regular surveys, signed by three officers, one at least to be commissioned, that the loss has been unavoidably sustained by damage, and not by any neglect or inattention on his part.

ART. 9. And as a compensation for the risk and responsibility, the purser shall be authorized to dispose of the slops to the crew at a profit of ten per cent; but he must, at the end of every cruise, render a regular slop account, showing by appropriate columns, the quantity of each article received or purchased, and the prices and amount, and from whom, when and where, and he shall show the quantity disposed of, and to whom, and at what prices, so that his slop account may show the articles' prices, and amounts received and disposed of.

ART. 10. When on foreign station there shall be a necessity to purchase slops, they are to be purchased agreeably to the established uniform of the navy, which in winter shall consist of a blue jacket and trowsers, and red vest, yellow buttons, and black hat. In summer the dress will be white duck jackets and trowsers, and vests; and on the home station they will be supplied from the navy stores, on requisition, in the same manner as other stores are supplied.

ART. 11. Slops are to be issued out publicly, and in the presence of an officer, who is to be appointed by the captain, to see the article delivered to the seamen and others, and the receipt given for the same, which he is also to certify. The captain is not to suffer any one to be supplied with slops except when absolutely necessary, and he is to oblige those who may be ragged, and in want of apparel or bedding, to receive such of these things as he shall stand in need of.

ART. 12. When any one dies on board, his clothes and other effects may be sold at auction, and the amount, after being charged to the buyer, shall be carried to the credit of the deceased, for the benefit of his legal representatives.

ART. 13. The purser shall be allowed a commission of five per cent, to be deducted from the amount of the sale of dead men's clothes.

ART. 14. No purser shall draw moneys at any time or place without the approval and signature of his commanding officer.

ART. 15. Captains or commanders may shorten the daily allowance of provisions when necessity shall require it.

ART. 16. No officer is to draw whole allowance while the ship's company is on short allowance.

ART. 17. Provisions and stores purchased by agents are to be surveyed when received on board; and if it should appear by the report of the surveying officers that they are unfit for public use, they are to be returned to the agents, and on settlement the captain is to refuse to admit them into the agent's accounts against the vessel, and is to transmit to the secretary of the navy a duplicate of the report of survey, with such remarks as the case may require.

ART. 18. Every cask and package of provisions, wet or dry, bread excepted, sent on board the Texian vessels of war, is to have the contents thereof, as to quantity and kind, distinctly marked on it, together with a number, and the time when, place where, and by whom purchased or furnished. The casks are to be marked on the head, and the packages on some proper or conspicuous part of them.

ART. 19. The resignation of any officer when called into active service will be considered a disobedience of orders.

NAVAL GENERAL COURTS MARTIAL.

ART. 1. General courts martial may be convened as often as the president of the republic of Texas, the secretary of the navy, or the commander-in-chief of the squadron, while out of the limits of the republic of Texas, shall deem it necessary; *provided*, that no general courts martial shall consist of more than nine, nor less than five members; and as many officers shall be summoned on every such court as can be convened without injury to the service, so as not to exceed nine; and the senior officer shall always preside, the others ranking agreeably to the date of their commissions; and in no case, when it can be avoided, without injury to the service, shall more than one half of the members, exclusive of the president, be junior to the officer to be tried.

ART. 2. Each member of the court martial, before proceeding to trial, shall take the following oath or affirmation, which the judge advocate, or person officiating as such is hereby authorized to administer:

> "I, A. B., do swear (or affirm) that I will truly try, without prejudice or partiality, the case now depending, according to the evidence which shall come before the court, the rules for the government of the navy, and my own conscience; and that I will not, by any means, divulge or disclose the sentence of the court until it shall have been approved by the proper authority; nor will I, at any time, divulge or disclose the vote or opinion of any particular member of the court unless required so to do before a court of justice, in due course of law."

ART. 3. All testimony given to a general court martial shall be on oath or affirmation, which the president of the court is hereby authorized to administer; and if any person shall refuse to give his evidence as aforesaid, or shall prevaricate, or shall behave with contempt to the court, it shall, and may be lawful, for the court to imprison such offender, at their discretion: *provided*, that the imprisonment in no case shall exceed two months, and every person who shall commit wilful perjury on examination on oath or affirmation before such court, or who shall corruptly procure or suborn any person to commit such wilful perjury, shall, and may be prosecuted by indictment or information, in any court of justice in the republic of Texas, and shall suffer such penalties as are authorized by the laws of the republic of Texas, in case of perjury or the subornation thereof. And in every prosecution for perjury or subornation, under this act, it shall be sufficient to set forth the offence charged on the defendant, without setting forth the authority by which the court was held, or the particular matters brought, or intended to be brought before the said court.

ART. 4. All charges on which an application for a general court martial is founded, shall be exhibited in writing to the proper officer, and the person demanding the court shall take care that the person accused shall be furnished with a true copy of the charges, with the specifications, at the time he is put under arrest; nor shall any other charge or charges, than those so exhibited, be urged against the person so to be tried before the court, unless it appear to the court that the intelligence of such charge had not reached the person demanding the court, when the person so to be tried was put under arrest, or that some witness, material to the support of such charge, who was at that time absent, can be produced; in which case, reasonable time shall be given to the person to be tried, to make his defence against such new charge. Every officer so arrested is to deliver up his sword to his commanding officer, and to confine himself to the limits assigned him, under pain of dismission from the service.

ART. 5. When the proceedings of any general court martial shall have commenced, they shall not be suspended or delayed, on account of the absence of any of the members: *provided* five or more be assembled; but the court is enjoined to sit from day to day, (Sundays excepted) until sentence be given: and no member of said court shall, after the proceedings are begun, absent himself therefrom, unless in case of sickness, or orders to go on duty, from a superior officer, on pain of being cashiered.

ART. 6. Whenever a court martial shall sentence an officer to be suspended, the court shall have power to suspend his pay and emoluments, for the whole, or any part of the time of his suspension.

ART. 7. All sentences of courts martial, which shall extend to the *loss of life*, shall require the concurrence of two thirds of the members present; and no such sentence shall be carried into execution, until confirmed by the president of the republic of Texas; or if the trial take place out of the limits of the republic of Texas, until it be confirmed by the commander of the squadron; all other sentences may be determined by a majority of votes, and carried into execution on confirmation of the commander of the fleet or squadron, or officer ordering the court, except such as go to the dismission of a commissioned or warrant officer, which are first to be approved by the president of the republic of Texas.

ART. 8. A court martial shall not, for any one offence not capital, inflict a punishment beyond one hundred lashes.

ART. 9. The president of the republic of Texas, or when the trial takes place out of the limits of Texas, the commander of the squadron, shall possess full powers to pardon any offence committed against these articles, after conviction, or to mitigate the punishment decreed by a court martial.

ART. 10. *And be it further enacted*, That courts of enquiry may be ordered by the president of the republic of Texas, the secretary of the navy, or the commander of the squadron: *provided* such court shall not consist of more than three members, who shall be commissioned officers, and a judge advocate, or person to do duty as such; and such courts shall have power to summon witnesses, administer oaths, and punish contempt, in the same manner as courts martial; but such courts shall merely state facts, and not give their opinion, unless expressly required so to do in the order for convening; and the party whose conduct shall be the subject of inquiry, shall have permission to cross examine all the witnesses.

ART. 11. The proceedings of courts of enquiry shall be authenticated by the signature of the president of the court, and judge advocate, and shall, in all cases not capital, or extending to dismission of a commissioned, or warrant officer, be evidence before a court martial: *provided* oral testimony cannot be obtained.

ART. 12. The judge advocate, or person officiating as such, shall administer to the members the following oath or affirmation: "You do swear (or affirm) well and truly to examine and enquire, according to the evidence, into the matter now before you, without partiality or prejudice." After which the president shall administer to the judge advocate, or person officiating as such, the following oath or affirmation: "You do swear (or affirm) truly to record the proceedings of this court, and the evidence to be given in the case in hearing."

REGULATIONS RELATIVE TO NAVAL SURGEONS AND THEIR ASSISTANTS.

ART. 1. Every naval surgeon, on being ordered to a vessel of war of the republic of Texas, shall, without delay, report himself to the commanding officer, and take in his charge all the medicines, instruments, hospital stores, utensils, and all other articles ordered for the use of the sick, agreeably to estimate, for which he shall give duplicate receipts to the medical purveyor, by whom they were supplied. He shall personally examine the articles before he passes his receipts, as he will be held strictly accountable for the expenditures thereof.

ART. 2. He shall keep, or cause to be kept, a regular account of the receipt and expenditure of the said articles of medicine, according to form; and at the expiration of every month, the amount of the hospital stores shall be carried to the credit side. These books he is carefully to preserve, and at the end of every year, to deliver them to the medical purveyor of the depot where he may have arrived.

ART. 3. Should a fresh supply of medicines, or other articles in the surgeon's department, be required on a foreign station, in consequence of any extraordinary number of sick, or by any injury sustained in a gale of wind, or in action, he shall make out a requisition for such articles as he may think absolutely necessary for the remainder of the cruise, or until he shall arrive in Texas; which requisition, when signed by the commander, shall be forwarded to the navy agent, or consul of the port where the vessel may be, who will direct the supply thereof. The surgeon shall examine and approve the accounts of all articles thus supplied, before they are received on board.

ART. 4. No condemnation of any article of medicine, or hospital stores, shall take place, unless a survey shall have been had on the same, by order of the commander, at the request of the surgeon. A lieutenant, one surgeon and mate, shall be appointed for this purpose, and their certificate shall be necessary to exonerate the naval surgeon from the responsibility which these regulations impose on him.

ART. 5. He shall prescribe for *casual cases*, on the gun deck, every morning at nine o'clock, due notice having been previously given by his lob-lolly boy, by ringing of a bell. He shall visit those who are confined to the sick berths twice a day, or oftener if necessary, and prescribe such medicines and diet as he may think proper; he shall likewise direct the stoppage or the rations of every man on the sick list and excused from duty, when he shall issue hospital stores in lieu thereof.

ART. 6. He shall cause the patients under his care to be removed to the sick berth, whenever he shall judge it expedient. He is to request the commander to order as many men as may be requisite to attend their companions, day and night, as nurses; and whilst engaged in this duty they shall be subject to the orders of the surgeon, unless when mustered, or called to quarters; should they neglect to perform the duties required, and not use tenderness and humanity in the performance of them, the surgeon shall make a proper representation thereof to the captain. The sick berth shall be supplied with a sufficient number of buckets with covers, for the use of the sick, which shall be emptied frequently, and cleansed, and charcoal and water put in them. The berth shall be whitewashed with lime, whenever an opportunity offers, and the deck sprinkled with vinegar.

ART. 7. He shall be extremely attentive to the personal cleanliness of the patients under his care, and see that the beds and bedding are properly attended to; also, that the sick are supplied with such medicines, drinks, and nourishments as their situation may require.

ART. 8. He shall report daily to the commander, the number, names, quality, and state of the sick under his care, then disease, and probable cause of the increase of the sick; also, the result of his treatment, agreeably to form. He shall likewise deposit in the binnacle, an alphabetical list of those who are, or ought to be, excused from duty, in consequence of wounds, disease, or other injuries.

ART. 9. The day previous to the discharge of a man from the sick report, *who has been subsisted by him*, he shall inform the purser in writing, in order that his steward may include him in his mess, in serving out the rations.

ART. 10. He shall at all times be prepared with everything necessary for the relief of wounded men; and when the vessel is cleared for action, he shall repair to the cock pit, with his assistants and attendants, or to such part of the vessel as the surgeon, with the consent of the commander, may consider most proper for their reception, the situation having been previously arranged.

ART. 11. A variety of cases may occur, when, for the preservation of the lives of the sick, as well as for the safety of those who are well, it may be conceived necessary to remove part of the sick on the gun deck; it is therefore deemed proper that he should recommend their removal whenever circumstances may make it necessary.

ART. 12. When sick or wounded men be sent to any of the naval hospitals of Texas, they shall be accompanied by an officer, and an assistant surgeon, to see that they are conveyed with all the care and comfort that circumstances will admit of.

ART. 13. Each man sent to the hospital shall be furnished with a sick ticket, also an inventory of his effects, agreeable to form.

ART. 14. Whenever very important and difficult cases occur, he shall, if practicable, consult with the surgeons of the fleet or squadron.

ART. 15. He shall instruct his assistants, and all others stationed with him, in the use of the tourniquet, and such other persons as the commander may appoint. A number of tourniquets shall be distributed to the different quarters; also, two or three to each top, that the wounded men may suffer as little as possible from the loss of blood, before their removal to the cock pit.

ART. 16. He shall occasionally inspect the crew, and take every precaution to prevent the origin or progress of contagion, on the appearance of which he shall, without delay, report the case to the commander, in order that a timely separation may be made of the sick from the well, and adopt such measures as may have a tendency to arrest the progress of the disease.

ART. 17. He shall frequently inspect the provisions and liquors which may be served out, and report the same to the commander, when unsound; he shall likewise direct his mates to examine the cook's coppers, to see that he keeps them clean, and likewise report every thing respecting diet, dress, want of personal cleanliness; in short, every thing which may come within the sphere of his knowledge, tending to promote the comfort and health of the crew.

ART. 18. He shall take care that the medicines, and all other articles with which he is supplied, are faithfully administered for the relief of the sick and wounded, and that no part of them be wasted or embezzled, or applied to any other purpose than that for which they were intended.

ART. 19. To enable the surgeon and his assistants to take proper care of the articles belonging to the medical department, a store room shall be allotted for their reception, which shall be solely under the charge of the surgeon, or, during his absence, of the first assistant.

ART. 20. Whenever the surgeon shall consider that a supply of fresh provisions, vegetables, or lemons, is necessary for the crew generally, he is to signify the same to the commanding officer.

ART. 21. The surgeon shall be allowed a faithful attendant to issue, under his direction, all supplies of provisions and hospital stores, and to attend to the preparations of the nourishment for the sick.

ART. 22. The purser shall, from time to time, supply, on the requisition of the surgeon, approved by the captain or commander, such articles of provisions as he may want for the use of the sick or convalescent; which articles shall be charged to the medical department, or against the rations of the sick which may have been stopped.

ART. 23. At the end of every six months, the surgeon shall report to the secretary of the navy, the conduct of his mates; whether they have performed their duty with zeal and industry.

Surgical instruments are to be delivered to the surgeon, and charged to his account; and on his removal from the vessel, he is to take a receipt from his successor, the medical purveyor, or the surgeon of the hospital where the vessel may be laid up; which receipt, when approved by the captain, shall acquit him front further responsibility respecting them.

THE GUNNER.

ART. 1. The gunner, having received directions for that purpose from the captain, is to inform the officer having charge of the ordnance, when the vessel will be ready to receive her guns. He is to attend to receive them on board, and to see that every gun is placed on its proper carriage, and put in good order for use.

ART. 2. He is to examine very carefully into the state of the magazine, that he may be certain of its being perfectly fitted, and perfectly dry, before the powder is carried on board; but if he should find any appearance of dampness, he is to report it to the captain that it may be properly dried.

ART. 3. He is to inform the captain when the powder will be ready to be sent on board, that the fire in the galley may be put out, before the vessel which carries it is suffered to come along side; while the powder is taking into the vessel, no candles are to be kept lighted, except those in the light room, nor is any man to be allowed to smoke tobacco: as soon as the whole is stored in the magazine, the gunner is to see the doors, the light room, and the scuttle carefully secured; and is to deliver the keys to the captain, or to such other officer as he shall appoint to take care of them.

ART. 4. He is never to keep any quantity of powder in any other part of the vessel than the magazine, except that which that captain shall order to be kept in the powder boxes or powder horns on deck;

and when he delivers cartridges from the magazine, he is to be very particular that they are in cases, properly shut; and whenever it may be necessary to move powder from the vessel, he is to use the utmost caution, that all the passages to the magazine may be welted, so as to prevent accident.

ART. 5. He is to turn the barrels of powder once at least in every three months, to prevent the separation of the nitre from the other ingredients of the powder. He is also to examine frequently the barrels, and if he should find any of them defective, he is to remove the powder into some of the barrels which have been emptied. He is frequently to examine the cartridges which are filled, that he may remove the powder from any of them which he may find defective.

ART. 6. When powder of various qualities shall be sent on board, he is to be very attentive in using them in the order which shall be prescribed.

ART. 7. He is frequently to examine into the state of the guns, their locks and carriages, that they may be immediately repaired or exchanged, if found defective; and he is frequently to examine the musketry, and all the other small arms, to see that they are kept clean, and in every respect fit for service.

ART. 8. He is to be attentive in keeping the shot racks full of shot, the powder horns and boxes of priming tubes full, and a sufficient quantity of match primed, and ready for being lighted at the shortest notice.

ART. 9. When a vessel is preparing for battle, he is to be particularly attentive to see that all the quarters are supplied with every thing necessary for the service of the guns, the boarders, firemen, &c. He is to see all the screens thoroughly wetted, and hung round the hatchways, and from them to the magazine, before he opens the magazine doors.

ART. 10. After an engagement he is to apply to the captain for a survey on the powder, shot, and other stores remaining under his charge, that the quantity expended in the engagement may be ascertained.

ART. 11. He is never to allow any match to be burnt in the day time, nor more than two lengths at the same time in the night, without an order from the captain. When a match is burning, it is always to hang over a tub of water, and the gunner's mate of the watch is to attend to it.

ART. 12. He is to take every possible precaution to prevent any ball cartridges being given to the men, among the blank cartridges issued for exercise.

ART. 13. He is to be very attentive to the conduct of the armorer and his mates, to see that they discharge their duty properly, that they keep the muskets and other small arms clean, and in good order, always repairing them when they are defective, and not suffering them, through neglect, to become too bad to be repaired.

ART. 14. As the brass sheves and iron pins of blocks of gun tackles, from being much exposed to salt water, are frequently set fast with rust, he is to be particularly attentive when this is the case, to cause the iron pins to be knocked out, and to be oiled and greased.

SURVEYS.

ART. 1. If any officer shall wilfully sign any false report of quantity and condition of stores or provisions he is ordered to survey, or shall discover any fraudulent practices in the management of such stores or provisions, without making proper mention of them in his report; or if any person shall give false account of stores or provisions, by which the surveying officer may be deceived, and be led to make out an improper report, he is to be immediately suspended, and his misconduct reported to the commander-in-chief, or to the secretary of the navy, that he may he tried by a court martial.

SAIL MAKER.

ART. 1. The sail maker is very carefully to examine the sails when they are received on board, and to inform the boatswain if he discover any defects in them, or any mistake in their number or dimensions; he is to examine carefully whether they are perfectly dry when they are put into the sail room; and if any part of them be damp, the first proper opportunity must be taken to dry them.

ART. 2. He is to be attentive to see all the sails properly tallied, and so disposed of in the sail rooms as to enable him to find immediately any that may be wanted.

ART. 3. He is frequently to inspect the condition of the sails in the sail rooms, to see that they are not injured by leak or vermin, and he is to report to the boatswain when it shall be necessary to have them taken upon deck to be dried. He is to repair them whenever they require it, and to use his best endeavours to keep them always lit for service.

CARPENTER.

ART. 1. When a vessel of war belonging to the republic of Texas is to be commissioned, the carpenter is to inspect very minutely into the state of the masts and yards, as well as those which may be in store, to insure their being perfectly sound, and in good order; he is also to examine every part of the hull, the magazine, store rooms and cabins, and he is to report to the captain any defect which he may discover.

ART. 2. He is to make every possible exertion in getting the stores on board, and he is to be very particular in observing that they are all perfectly good, and that he receives his full allowance of every article.

ART. 3. When the vessel shall be at sea, he is once at least every day to examine into the state of the masts and yards, and to report to the officer of the watch when he discovers any of them to be sprung, or to be in any way defective.

ART. 4. In vessels of two decks, he is frequently to examine the lower deck ports, to see that they are properly lined, and when they are barred in, he and his mates are frequently to see that they are properly secured.

ART. 5. He is to be particularly careful in keeping the pumps in good order, always having at hand whatever may be necessary to repair them.

ART. 6. He is to keep the boats, ladders, and gratings, in as good condition as possible, always repairing every damage they may sustain as soon as he discovers it.

ART. 7. He is to keep always ready, for immediate use, shot plugs, and every other article necessary for stopping shot holes, and repairing other damages in battle; and, during the action, he is, with the part of the crew appointed to assist him, to be continually going about the wings and passages, and the hold, to discover where shot may have passed through, that he may plug up the holes and stop the leaks, as expeditiously as possible.

ART. 8. If he should at any time find stores, or other articles stowed in the wings or passages, in such a manner as might interfere with his working, if required to cut out shot, or stop leaks during an action, he is to report it to the captain, that they may be removed.

ART. 9. When the vessel is going into port, he is to prepare as correct an account as possible of the defect of the hull, masts and yards, and of the repairs she may stand in need of, of which he is to deliver to the captain two copies, one of which, when signed by the captain, he is to deliver to the master shipwright of the station. In making this report he is to be very careful not to exaggerate any defect, by which there may appear to be a greater necessity for the vessel's being repaired than really exists, nor is he to conceal any which may require to he repaired.

BOATSWAIN.

ART. 1. When a Texian vessel is commissioned, the boatswain is to exert himself to get on board all the stores committed to his charge, as expeditiously as possible; he is to examine them very carefully, and to inspect very minutely all fitted rigging, and to report to the captain such defects as he may discover in them.

ART. 2. When fitting out the vessel, and at all other times when it may be necessary to cut out rigging, he is to be extremely careful to cut every rope of the precise length allowed by the establishment, unless some particular circumstance, appertaining to the vessel, shall make it necessary to alter it; in which case he is to inform the captain, and to receive his orders for such alteration.

ART. 3. He is, once at least every day, to examine the state of the rigging, to discover, as soon as possible, any part which may be chafed, or likely to give way, that it may be repaired without loss of time. He is at all times to be very careful that the anchors, booms, and boats be properly secured.

ART. 4. He is to be very particular in having ready at all times, a sufficient number of mats, plats, nippers, points, and gaskets, that no delay may be experienced when they are wanted.

ART. 5. He is to be very attentive in observing, while junk is working up, that every part of it is converted to all such purposes as it can possibly be made applicable to.

ART. 6. He is to be very frequently on deck during the day, and at times both by day and night. When any duty shall require all hands to be employed, he is, with his mates, to see that the men go quickly upon deck when called, and that when there, they perform their duty with alacrity, and without noise or confusion.

ART. 7. When the vessel is preparing for battle, he is to be very particular in seeing that every thing necessary for repairing the rigging is in its proper place, that the men stationed for that service may know where to find immediately whatever may be wanted.

ART. 8. When the vessel is ordered to be paid off, he is to be very attentive to prevent any of the rigging being damaged or cut, and he is to see every part of it properly tallied and stopped together, before he returns it in stores.

CHAPLAIN.

ART. 1. He is to read prayers at stated periods, perform all funeral ceremonies over such persons as may die in the service in the vessel to which he belongs; or if directed by the commanding officer, over any person that may die in any other public vessel.

ART. 2. He shall perform the duty of schoolmaster, and to that end he shall instruct the midshipmen in, writing, arithmetic, and navigation, and in whatsoever may contribute to render them proficient. He is likewise to teach the other youths of the vessel according to such orders as he shall receive from the captain. He is to be diligent in his office.

ART. 3. He shall, when it is required of him, perform the duties of secretary to the commodore.

MIDSHIPMEN.

ART. 1. No particular duties can be assigned to this class of officers. They are promptly and faithfully to execute all the orders for the public service which they shall receive from the commanding officers.

ART. 2. The commanding officers will consider the midshipmen as a class of officers, meriting in an especial degree their fostering care. They will see, therefore, that the schoolmaster performs his duty towards them, by diligently and faithfully instructing them in those sciences appertaining to their profession, and that he use his utmost care to render them proficient therein.

ART. 3. Midshipmen are to keep regular journals, and deliver them to the commanding officer at the stated periods, in due form.

ART. 4. They are to consider it as a duty they owe to their country, to employ a due portion of their time in the study of naval tactics, and in acquiring a thorough knowledge of all the various duties to be performed on board a man of war.

MARINES SERVING ON BOARD THE VESSELS OF THE REPUBLIC OF TEXAS.

ART. 1. The marine detachments appointed to serve on board the vessels of the republic of Texas, are to be entered upon their books as part of the complements for victuals, and with regard to provisions, and short allowance money, they are to be in all respects upon the same footing with the seamen.

ART. 2. All marine officers are to obey the orders of the captain or commanding officer of the vessel, and also of the commanding officer of the watch. The marine officers are, upon all occasions, to be treated as well by the captain of the vessel as by all other officers and people belonging to her, with the respect, decency, and regard due to the commissions they bear. They are to possess the cabins or berths erected for them.

ART. 3. The marines are to be exercised by the marine officers in the use of their arms as often as possible, that they may become expert in the use thereof. They are to be employed as sentinels, and upon all other duties and service on board of the vessel which they may be capable of, and therein to be subject to the directions of the officers of the vessel; but they are not to be obliged to go aloft, or to be punished for not showing an inclination to do so. And the captain or commanding officer of the vessel is strictly charged not to suffer them to be ill treated, nor a sergeant or corporal to be struck on any account, by any of the officers, petty officers, or seamen.

ART. 4. No marine, serving on board of any of the Texian vessels of war, is to be discharged as such, and entered as a seaman, without special authority from the secretary of the navy.

ART. 5. The commanding marine officer is to have in his possession the chests prepared for the arms, and the cartridges for the use of the marines. The arms and drums are to be under his charge, and he is to be accountable for any loss or damage that may happen for want of sufficient care in him; but if any such loss or damage happen by the default of any other person, the marine officer is immediately to acquaint the captain of the vessel therewith, who is to cause the value thereof to be forthwith noted against the defaulter's name, in order to its being deducted from his pay or wages.

ART. 6. The marine arms are to be kept clean and in good order by the marines themselves, so far as they can do the same; but if necessary, the marine officer may apply to the captain for the assistance of one or more armorer's mates, to repair the arms, and the captain in such case will order such assistance to be afforded.

ART. 7. When marines are sent on board of any of the Texian vessels in order to serve at sea, the captain of the vessel is to cause the purser to supply them, upon their coming on board, with a suit of bedding if necessary, and from time to time with such further bedding and slop clothes, &c., as the commanding marine officer may represent them to be in want of; for all which the officer charged with paying the marines shall settle with the purser of the vessel, charging the amount thereof to the accounts of the marines to whom such bedding and slops have been so issued.

ART. 8. The commanding marine officer on board must examine, once a week at least, into the state of the clothing and slops belonging to each marine, and if he finds any loss or abuse must enquire how it happened; and he is to inform the captain of the vessel of the circumstances, who will apply such corrective as may be necessary to prevent the recurrence of such losses or abuses.

ART. 9. When any marine belonging to the vessel dies, his clothing and effects (except his uniform marine clothing) are to be sold at the mast, by auction, and the proceeds charged against the names of the buyers: and the marine officer will, by the first opportunity, transmit to the paymaster of the marine corps, an inventory of the effects so sold, and an account of the money or amount for which they sold, signed by the captain and purser of the vessel, in order that such amount may be paid over to the legal representatives of the deceased.

ART. 10. A store room on board of each vessel to be in the possession of the marine officer, is to be appropriated exclusively for the spare clothing, accoutrements, and all other necessaries for the use of the marines.

ART. 11. Marines, sick or wounded are to be taken the same care of by the surgeon of the vessel, that the seamen are; and when it shall be necessary to send them out of the vessel for cure, they are to be sent on shore to the hospital or sick quarters, and are to be in all respects under the same regulations that are established for the seamen; sick tickets are to be sent with them, similar to those to be sent with seamen. The captain of the vessel and the commanding marine officer on board, are to see that their bedding, clothes, and necessaries are sent along with them, the particulars of which are to be noted at the foot of the sick tickets. The commanding marine officer will see that each man's things be securely bound together and labeled. The proper officer at the hospital, or sick quarters, and the marine officer attending hospital duty (when there shall be any) are to take care that the same be safely deposited and preserved, till the marines are either discharged, runaway, or die. If discharged they are to be delivered to their respective owners, and in the cases of desertion or death, they are to be disposed of as provided in the case of dead men's clothes on board of vessels.

ART. 12. Marines sent sick on shore, are to be continued upon the books of the vessel from which they shall be sent, unless the proportion of marines allowed the vessel be completed during their sickness; and in the latter case they are, when recovered, to be turned over to some other vessel wanting marines, or to be sent to the nearest marine station. So soon as the number allowed the vessel be completed, all marines sent sick on shore are to be discharged from the ship's books, as the vessel must never be charged with more than the complement of marines allowed her.

ART. 13. When a marine is returned on ship board from a hospital or sick quarters, the captain of the vessel is to take care that there be charged against his name the value of any clothing he may have been supplied with at the hospital, which the hospital surgeon is to set off upon the ticket of discharge from the hospital.

ART. 14. The rations issued to the marines must be charged by the purser to the subsistence of marine corps, in order that the subsistence of the navy may have credit therefor in the settlement of his account.

ART. 15. Marines are to be paid by the purser of the vessel while they are on board, and charged the same as the vessel's crew. Pay rolls signed by the purser, and countersigned by the marine officer, are to be regularly transmitted to the auditor of the treasury.

NAVY AGENTS.

ART. 1. The navy agent being the person appointed to purchase supplies for the service of the navy, pay bills, and sell off all surplus or useless stores, is required to observe and abide by the following regulations, stipulations, and instructions, as well as such instructions of other officers detailed in this volume, as have a bearing upon the duties assigned to him; and he is not to expect that any irregularity or omission in the filling up of the several forms referred to herein, for the keeping of his accounts, will pass unnoticed.

ART. 2. All supplies for vessels repairing at the navy yard, or in ordinary, are to be furnished by the agents on the requisition of the commander.

ART. 3. Stores, provisions, and supplies of every description, purchased by an agent for the naval service of Texas, are to be obtained at the lowest rates, and of the best quality; and upon the presentment of his accounts at the treasury department, he must produce such account attested by the signature of the commanding officer, in proof of accuracy. He must also produce, at the same time, the different requisitions which were made upon him for supplies, signed and countersigned, in proof of his authority for purchases: and lastly, he must exhibit the receipts of the respective officers to whom the supplies were delivered. Without each and every of these documents, his accounts shall not be settled, nor shall he receive a credit for any account not vouched as above required.

ART. 4. All articles sent on board public vessels, by an agent, are to be delivered to the commanding officer, or such person as he may authorize to receive them, otherwise their delivery shall be at the risk of the agent.

ART. 5. Provisions and stores, purchased by an agent, are to be surveyed when received on board; and if it appears by the report of the surveying officer, that they are unfit for the service, they are to be returned to the agent, and, on settlement, the captain is to refuse to admit them in the account against the vessel, and to transmit to the secretary of the navy a duplicate of the report of survey, accompanied by such remarks as the case may make necessary.

ART. 6. Every cask and package of provisions or supplies, (bread excepted) wet or dry, must be numbered, and have the contents thereof distinctly marked on it, as to quantity and kind, as well as the time when, place where, and by whom purchased or furnished. The casks are to be marked on the head, and the packages on some proper and conspicuous part of them.

ART. 7. Every navy agent must forward his accounts with the

necessary vouchers for settlement, to the auditor of the treasury, quarterly, to wit: On the first days of January, April, July, and October; in which must be distinctly stated the moneys expended, and articles furnished for each vessel, and for other purposes. He will also be required to exhibit an account of the articles purchased and remaining in his possession, of those delivered over for sale; a statement of the sales of old or unserviceable articles, and a particular account of the moneys unexpended, and remaining in his hands.

ART. 8. No moneys are to be paid over by an agent, no purchases, or sales made, nor any expenses incurred, except with the knowledge and sanction of the commanding officer of the squadron, or under particular instructions from the secretary of the navy.

ART. 9. Every agent who shall, for two successive quarters, neglect to send in his accounts for settlement, as required unless specially exempted by the secretary of the navy, shall, from thenceforward, not be allowed any of the emoluments appertaining to the office he holds; and if he neglects for three successive quarters to send them in, his powers as agent shall totally cease, and his commission be null and void.

ART. 10. Agents shall not be concerned directly or indirectly in any supplies which it may be their duty to furnish the navy; and if it shall be found that they have participated in the profits of any such supplies, they shall be dismissed from their offices, and will be prosecuted to the amount of their bonds.

ART. 11. Navy agents shall not advance money to pursers or other officers of a vessel, when destined on service, unless by and with the previous sanction of the secretary of the navy, by whom the amount shall be limited.

ART. 12. Navy agents shall transmit quarterly to the secretary of the navy, viz: On the first days of January, April, July, and October, of each year, a statement of all purchases turned into stores, accompanied by the store keeper's receipt for the same.

CAPTIVES AND PRIZE MONEY.

ART. 1. *And be it further enacted*, That all pay and emoluments of such officers and men of any of the vessels of the republic of Texas taken by an enemy, who shall appear, by the sentence of a court martial, or otherwise, to have done their utmost to preserve and defend their vessel, and after the taking thereof, have behaved themselves obediently to their superiors, agreeably to the discipline of the navy, shall go on and be paid there, until their death, their exchange, or discharge.

ART. 2. *And be it further enacted*, That the proceeds of all the vessels, and the goods taken on board of them, which shall be adjudged good prize, shall, when of equal or superior force to the vessel making the capture, be the sole property of the captors; and when of inferior force, shall be divided equally between the government of Texas, and the officers and men making the capture.

ART. 3. *And be it enacted*, That the prize money belonging to the officers and men shall be distributed in the following manner:

1st – To the commanding officers of a squadron, or a single vessel, three twentieths, of which the commanding officer of the squadron shall have one twentieth, if the prize be taken by a vessel under his command; and the commander of a single vessel two twentieths; but when a prize is taken by a vessel acting independently of such superior officer, the three twentieths shall belong to the commander.

2d – To sea lieutenants, captains of marines, and sailing masters, two twentieths; but when there is a captain, without a lieutenant of marines, these officers shall be entitled to two twentieths and one third of a twentieth, which third, in such cases shall be deducted from the share of the officers mentioned in article number 3 of this section.

3d – To chaplains, lieutenants of marines, surgeons, pursers, boatswains, gunners, carpenters, and masters' mates, two twentieths.

4th – To midshipmen, surgeon's mates, captain's clerk, schoolmaster, boatswain's mates, gunner's mates, carpenter's mates, ship's stewards, sail makers, master-at-arms, armorers, cockswains and coopers, three twentieths and a half.

5th – To gunner's yeoman, boatswain's yeoman, quartermasters, quarter gunners, sail maker's mates, sergeants and corporals of marines, drummers, fifers, and extra petty officers, two twentieths and a half.

6th — To seamen, ordinary seamen, marines, and all other persons doing duty on board, seven twentieths.

7th — Whenever one or more public vessels are in sight, at the time any one or more vessels are taking a prize or prizes, they shall all share equally in the prize or prizes, according to the number of men and guns on board each vessel in sight.

IRA INGRAM,
Speaker of the house of representatives.
RICHARD ELLIS,
President pro tem. of the senate.

Approved Dec. 15, 1836.

SAM. HOUSTON.

AN ACT,

To incorporate the Texas Rail Road, Navigation, and Banking Company.

SEC. 1. *Be it enacted by the senate and house of represents lives of the republic of Texas, in congress assembled*, That Messrs. Branch T. Archer, James Collinsworth, and their present and future associates, successors, and assigns, be, and they are hereby ordained, constituted, and declared to be, from and immediately after the passage of this act, a body corporate and politic, in fact and in name, by the style and title of the "TEXAS RAIL-ROAD, NAVIGATION, AND BANKING COMPANY;" and by that name, they and their successors, shall and may have continual succession, and shall be persons in law, capable of suing and being sued, pleading and being impleaded, answering and being answered unto, defending and being defended, in all courts and places whatsoever; and that they and their successors may have a common seal, and may change and alter the same at pleasure; and also, that they and their successors, by the same name and style, shall be in law capable of holding, purchasing, and conveying any estate, real, personal, or mixed, for the use of the said corporation, and doing and performing all things which are necessary and common for companies of a similar nature to do, not contrary to the provisions of this charter, as hereinafter enacted, or to the constitution of this republic.

SEC. 2. *Be it further enacted*, That the said company shall have

x

LAWS

banking privileges, with a capital stock of five millions of dollars, as well as the right of connecting the waters of the Rio Grande and the Sabine, by means of internal navigation and railroads, from and to such particular points of connection as may be agreed upon and selected by said company, with a privilege also of constructing such branches, either by canals or railroads, to connect with the main line above named, as may be agreed upon and determined by said company.

SEC. 3. *Be it further enacted*, That the capital stock of said company, shall be five millions of dollars, and be divided into fifty thousand shares, of one hundred dollars each; and that Messrs. Branch T. Archer, James Collinsworth, and their present associates, be, and are hereby appointed directors of said company; and whose duty it shall be to do and perform all the business incumbent upon them as such, necessary to the successful operation of said bank, and the completion of said works; and the same shall continue in office until their successors shall be duly elected and qualified.

SEC. 4. *Be it further enacted*, That the aforesaid directors, their successors or assigns, shall have full power to borrow money upon the faith of this charter, and also to pledge such property, real or personal, of their own, for the payment of the same, as in their wisdom may best conduce to the interest of said corporation; and also to do and perform, as directors of said bank, every thing necessary and proper in carrying it into complete operation; which said bank shall not go into operation until it has a specie capital of one million of dollars paid in. And it shall not be lawful for said bank to charge more, upon any paper, bond, or note by it discounted, than ten per cent, per annum; but shall have the privilege of buying and selling bills of exchange, at such rates as the market may afford for the time being; and that the said directors shall have full power to enact such by-laws, rules, and regulations, for the government of said bank, and the works therewith connected, as they may deem necessary for the use and protection of the same, and for the election of directors and all other matters.

SEC. 5. *Be it further enacted*, That upon the going into operation of said bank, said company shall pay over to the treasurer of Texas a *bonus*, in gold or silver, as shall be required, the sum of twenty-five thousand dollars, and also two and one-half per cent, per annum,

141

upon the net profits arising from the tolls, fees, and charges, of such canals and rail-roads as may be constructed, so long as such charter shall continue; and also the said government or republic of Texas, shall have a free privilege of transporting all soldiers, provisions, ammunitions, and munitions of war, and also all transports and ships of war, free of tolls or other charges.

SEC. 6. *Be it further enacted*, That said charter shall continue in full force and virtue, for and during the period of forty-nine years from the passage of this act, at the end of which time the said company shall have the privilege of renewing the same for a like period, by paying to the government five hundred thousand dollars in gold or silver, and by further paying thereafter of five per cent, per annum, upon the net profits arising upon all tolls, fees, and charges of said works.

SEC. 7. *Be it further enacted*, That so soon as said bank shall go into operation, it shall be the duty of said company to commence said improvements, and complete the same as soon thereafter as the means of said company will permit.

SEC. 8. *Be it further enacted*, That if, at any time from and after the passage of this act, in the opinion of the company, the commercial wants of the country, and the welfare of the company shall require it, said capital stock may be increased to the sum of ten millions of dollars, by paying over to the government or state of Texas, at that time, a further bonus of one hundred thousand dollars: *provided*, in no instance shall said company discount more than three dollars to one upon the capital paid in: *and provided* furthermore, that upon failure of said bank to redeem promptly its issues in gold or silver, upon presentation, such of its bills as should be protested for non-payment according to law, shall, from the date of such protest, bear an interest of ten per cent, per annum, until paid, and for the payment of which, all the chartered property of said company shall be held responsible.

SEC 9. *Be it further enacted*, That any person or persons who may own lands through which said company shall wish to run said rail-roads or canals, and shall refuse to allow the same, said company may, by applying to the county court of the county in which said land may be situated, for a writ of ad quod damnum, directing the sheriff of said county to summon a jury of six freeholders, who shall assess the damage which said road or canal may cause, and award the same to the owner or owners of said lands, and upon the payment, by the company, either to the sheriff of said county, or to the party so refusing, such award, together with the sum of two dollars per day for each of the jurymen, for each and every day so employed, and ten dollars to the sheriff, shall thereby have a good and bona fide title to such land, stone, timber, or other building materials, as shall be awarded; and should the said company wish to occupy any portion of the public lands, by their improvements, they shall have the right to take possession of, and pay to the government the minimum price of such lands, provided however, that said company shall not be permitted to occupy more than one half mile of such public land from their works, on either side.

SEC. 10. *Be it further enacted*, That if any person or persons whatsoever, shall wilfully, by any means whatever, injure, molest, or destroy any part of the roads or canals constructed by said company under this act, or any of their works, buildings, fixtures, or machines, or other property, such person or persons so offending shall, each of them, be liable for all damages occasioned thereby; and at any time within twelve months after such offence shall have been committed, and upon conviction, be punished by a fine not exceeding ten thousand dollars, or imprisonment not exceeding twelve months, or both, at the discretion of the court.

SEC. 11. *Be it further enacted*, That the said company shall have the power to locate the bank at such place as they may think proper, and to establish as many branches thereof as they may think the necessities of the community require.

SEC. 12. *Be it further enacted*, That the executive shall annually appoint a government commissioner, whose business it shall be to examine into the circumstances of said corporation, and report thereon, whether the government bonus has been properly made out and paid over to the proper officer of the government, to receive the same. The pay of said commissioner, to be hereafter determined by some future congress, to be paid by said institution.

SEC. 13. *Be it further enacted*, That in the event the first named bonus of twenty-five thousand dollars, shall not be paid within eighteen months from and after the passage of this act, the said charter shall be forfeited, and forever thereafter be null and void.

SEC. 14. *And be it further enacted*, That said company shall not issue any note for a smaller sum than five dollars, neither shall they establish more than two branches without the consent of some future congress, and they shall pay one per cent upon the dividends of said Bank for the use of the republic.

IRA INGRAM,
Speaker of the house of representatives.
RICHARD ELLIS,
President pro tem. of the senate.

Approved Dec. 16, 1836.

SAM. HOUSTON.

JOINT RESOLUTION,

For the relief of John Ricord.

Resolved, by the senate and house of representatives of the republic of Texas, in congress assembled, That the secretary of the treasury be, and he is hereby authorized and required to pay John Ricord, out of any moneys in the treasury not otherwise appropriated, at the rate of fifteen hundred dollars per annum for the time he acted as private secretary to the president "ad interim," and also for the time he has acted as such to the present incumbent.

IRA INGRAM,
Speaker of the house of representatives.
RICHARD ELLIS,
President pro tem. of the senate.

Approved Dec. 17, 1836.

SAM. HOUSTON.

JOINT RESOLUTION,

For the relief of Thomas J. Green.

Resolved, by the senate and house of representatives of the republic of Texas, in congress assembled, That the president be, and he is hereby authorized to pay to Thomas J. Green or order, out of the first means in the treasury, or any agency of Texas, the sum of twenty-four thousand one hundred and fifty-four dollars and four cents, say

$24,154.04, together with the damages and cost of protest for and on account of this government: *provided*, he, the said Thomas J. Green, shall file with the executive the account of the same, reported to this congress receipted in full.

IRA INGRAM,
Speaker of the house of representatives.
RICHARD ELLIS,
President pro tem. of the senate.
Approved Dec. 17, 1836.

SAM. HOUSTON.

————

JOINT RESOLUTION,

Requiring the Chief Justices of the County Courts to give information to the Secretary of State, concerning the boundaries of their respective counties.

Resolved, by the senate and house of representatives of the republic of Texas, in congress assembled, That the chief justices of the several county courts of this republic be, and they are hereby required to furnish the secretary of state with a description of their county boundaries, and such other information and observations relative to the same, as they may conceive conducive to the convenience of their citizens, and said information is required to be furnished by the first day of May next.

IRA INGRAM,
Speaker of the house of representatives.
RICHARD ELLIS,
President pro tem. of the senate.
Approved Dec. 17, 1836.

SAM. HOUSTON.

————

AN ACT,

To define the Boundaries of the Republic of Texas.

SEC. 1. *Be it enacted by the senate and house of representatives of the republic of Texas, in congress assembled,* That from and after the passage of this act, the civil and political jurisdiction of this republic be, and is hereby declared to extend to the following boundaries, to wit:

beginning at the mouth of the Sabine river, and running west along
the Gulf of Mexico three leagues from land, to the mouth of the Rio
Grande, thence up the principal stream of said river to its source,
thence due north to the forty-second degree of north latitude,
thence along the boundary line as defined in the treaty between the
United States and Spain, to the beginning: and that the president be,
and is hereby authorized and required to open a negotiation with the
government of the United States of America, so soon as in his
opinion the public interest requires it, to ascertain and define the
boundary line as agreed upon in said treaty.

IRA INGRAM,
Speaker of the house of representatives.
RICHARD ELLIS,
President of the senate pro tem.
Approved Dec. 19, 1836.
SAM. HOUSTON.

———

AN ACT,

Authorizing the Printing and Publishing the Laws of the Provisional Government, the Acts of the Convention of March last and the present Congress.

SEC. 1. *Be it enacted by the senate and house of representatives of the republic of Texas, in congress assembled,* That the president be, and he is
hereby authorized and required to cause to be printed in pamphlet
form, as soon as practicable, two thousand five hundred copies of
the laws and resolutions of the provisional government, together
with the constitution, ordinances and resolutions of the convention
of March last, and the acts, and two hundred and fifty copies of the
journals of the present congress: and that he furnish each judge,
justice of the peace, sheriff, clerks of the different courts, and
members of congress, with a copy as soon as practicable.

IRA INGRAM,
Speaker of the house of representatives.
RICHARD ELLIS,
President of the senate pro tem.
Approved Dec. 19, 1836.
SAM. HOUSTON.

JOINT RESOLUTION,

Making specific Appropriations.

SEC. 1. *Be it enacted by the senate and house of representatives of the republic of Texas, in congress assembled,* That the proceeds of the land scrip, and the sale of a league and labor of land on the east end of Galveston Island, which have or may come into the hands of our agent, David White of Mobile, be, and are hereby exclusively appropriated for the purpose of furnishing our army with supplies of clothing, provisions, and munitions of war: *provided* that the appropriations made by this resolution shall not be so construed as to affect any previous appropriations made by this congress out of said funds.

IRA INGRAM,
Speaker of the house of representatives.
RICHARD ELLIS,
President of the senate pro tem.

Approved Dec. 19, 1836.

SAM. HOUSTON.

AN ACT,

Establishing Fees of Office.

SEC. 1. *Be it enacted by the senate and house of representatives of the republic of Texas, in congress assembled,* That it shall be lawful for the clerks of the supreme court, clerks of the district courts, clerks of the county courts, clerks of the courts of probate, county recorders, judges of probate, justices of the peace, attorneys and counsellors at law, attorney general, notaries public, sheriffs, coroners, constables, and chief justices of the county courts respectively, to demand and receive the several fees hereinafter mentioned, for any business by them respectively done by virtue of their several offices, and no more; that is to say:

TO THE CLERKS OF THE SUPREME COURT,

For entering the appearance of either party in person or by attorney, fifty cents; for every rule entered on rule docket, fifty cents; for copy of every rule, seventy-five cents; for entering every continuance, one dollar; for administering an oath or affirmation, twenty-five cents; for docketing cause, to be charged but once, seventy-five cents; for entering every judgment, two dollars; for entering every decree, two dollars; for filing the record upon a writ of error, certiorari, or supersedeas, seventy-five cents; for taxing costs in any suit or action and copy thereof, one dollar; for every order in court, seventy-five cents; for a search for any thing above a year's standing and reading if required, fifty cents; for all copies required to be made, for every hundred words, twenty-five cents; for every service not herein mentioned, the same fees allowed the clerks of the district court for similar services; and there shall be allowed by the supreme court to their clerk, reasonable office rent, stationary, and tables, to be paid out of the treasury of the republic, on the order of the court.

TO THE CLERKS OF THE DISTRICT COURTS,

For each writ, with copy of petition, two dollars; for docketing each cause, to be charged but once, twenty-five cents; for filing each bond, declaration, plea, or other pleading or paper, twelve and a half cents; for entering each appearance, twenty-five cents; for entering each motion, rule, or order, thirty-seven and a half cents; for declaration in ejectment, three dollars; for entering each non-suit, discontinuance, or *nolle prosequi*, seventy-five cents; for order and copy of rule of reference, one dollar; for swearing each witness, twelve and a half cents; for entering each continuance, thirty-seven and a half cents; for venire facias, in every cause tried by jury, fifty-cents; for scire facias, (except against jurors when excused) two dollars; for swearing and empanelling every jury, fifty cents; for receiving and entering verdict, fifty cents; for entering each judgment, seventy-five cents; for each subpoena, for one witness, fifty cents; for every additional name inserted, twenty-five cents; for entering surrender of principal by his bail, fifty cents; for commission to take depositions, one dollar; for copy of interrogatories to accompany said commission, for every hundred words, twenty cents; for taking a recognizance, seventy-five cents; for each execution, one dollar; for taxing costs in each cause and copy of same, seventy-five cents; for making a complete record of any cause after final judgment, for every hundred words, twenty-five cents; for each bail, price seventy-five cents; for each certificate without seal, twenty-five cents; for each certificate with seal of office, fifty cents;

for entering finding of indictment or filing information, fifty cents; for arraigning prisoner and entering plea, one dollar and fifty cents; for all copies, other than herein mentioned, for every hundred words, twenty cents; for all services not herein provided for, such sum as the court shall direct; and there shall be allowed reasonable office rents, stationary, cases and tables, by the court, to be paid on the order of the court, out of the county treasury.

TO THE CLERKS OF THE COUNTY COURTS,

For like services by them performed, the same fees as are by law allowed to the clerks of the district courts.

TO THE CLERKS OF THE PROBATE COURTS,

For recording the probate of any will or testament, and for letters testamentary thereon, two dollars; for recording a will, testament, codicil, an inventory, appraisement for executors', administrators', collectors', or guardians' accounts, or any other papers than herein otherwise provided for, for every hundred words, twenty cents; for taking bond and administering oath to executors, administrators, collectors, or guardians, and recording the same, two dollars; for letters of administration, collection, or guardianship, and copy of order granting the same, two dollars; for all orders and copies not herein otherwise provided for, for every hundred words, twenty cents.

TO THE COUNTY RECORDERS,

For the oath of a witness or the acknowledgement of the party to the signature of any writing, and making certificate of the same, fifty cents; for all recording, and all copies from his office, for every hundred words, twenty cents.

TO JUDGES OF PROBATE,

For taking the probate of any will or testament, two dollars; for examining, stating, and reporting each account of executors, administrators, collectors, or guardians, one-half per cent, commission on the amount of such account; for appointing an administrator, collector, or guardian and appraiser, two dollars; for each order for the partition of real estate among heirs or devisees, one dollar; for each order for the appointment of commissioners on the representation of an estate being insolvent, one dollar; for apportionment of an insolvent's estate among creditors, five dollars.

TO JUSTICES OF THE PEACE,

For each warrant in civil cases, with copy of petition, one dollar; for each warrant in criminal cases, one dollar; for each judgment, seventy-five cents; for each mittimus or recognizance, seventy-five cents; for each subpoena for witnesses, twenty-five cents; for each execution, one dollar; for each attachment, including bond and affidavit, two dollars; for each appeal, with the proceedings, bond, and certificate, two dollars; for each oath or affidavit, twelve and a half cents; for each certificate, twenty-five cents; for taxing costs on any execution, twenty-five cents; for each transcript of his record, for every hundred words, twenty cents; for all writing required of him by virtue of his office, not herein otherwise provided for, for every hundred words, twenty cents.

TO ATTORNEYS AND COUNSELLORS AT LAW,

For prosecuting or defending a suit in supreme court, twenty-five dollars; for like services in a district court ten dollars; for like services in a county court, five dollars; for prosecuting or defending a real or mixed action, in supreme or district courts, thirty dollars; for each appeal from the decision of a justice of the peace to the county court, five dollars.

TO THE ATTORNEY GENERAL OR DISTRICT ATTORNEYS,

(For the use of the republic of Texas) for every criminal prosecution by indictment, in cases of felony, where the offender is convicted, fifty dollars; for every prosecution for misdemeanors, where the offender is convicted, ten dollars; for every action by original writ in behalf of the republic, for the recovery of a pecuniary penalty, where the defendant is convicted, ten dollars.

TO NOTARIES PUBLIC,

For protesting any bill, registering and seal, two dollars; for attesting letters of attorney and seal, one dollar; for notarial affidavit to an account or other writing and seal, fifty cents; for registering a foreign bill, protested with certificates, two dollars; for registering a protest of a bill of exchange or note for non-payment or non-acceptance, one dollar; for each oath or affirmation, with seal, fifty cents; for all other notarial acts not otherwise provided for, with seal, one dollar.

LAWS

TO SHERIFFS,

For levying an attachment on the estate of an absent or absconding debtor, two dollars; for serving each writ not herein otherwise provided for, two dollars; for levying execution, two dollars; for making money on execution, for the first hundred dollars, five per cent; for all sums over one hundred and not exceeding two hundred dollars, four percent; and for all sums above two hundred dollars, two and a half per cent; for returning execution, seventy-five cents; for serving defendant with copy of writ, fifty cents; for each bail, bond, or recognizance, and assignment thereof, one dollar; for summoning each witness, fifty cents; for executing a writ of possession and return, two dollars; for making a deed to purchasers of real estate, three dollars; for attending prisoner on habeas corpus, each day, three dollars; for each commitment or release, one dollar; for serving a declaration in ejectment, and copy thereof, two dollars; for taking a bond of any kind, fifty cents; for executing a death warrant, twenty-five dollars; for removing a prisoner, for every mile, going and returning, twelve and a half cents; for every day's attendance with such prisoner on the judge, in vacation, three dollars; for empanelling a jury, in each cause, where a jury is sworn, fifty cents; for whipping a free person by order of court, two dollars; for whipping a slave by order of court, one dollar; for branding by order of court, three dollars; for serving scire facias on each defendant, seventy-five cents; for serving an attachment for contempt and returning same, one dollar and twenty-five cents; for executing venire facias, to be taxed in each cause tried, fifty cents; for summoning a special jury, three dollars; for serving every person with a summons, not herein provided for, fifty cents; where property attached is sold, the same commissions as for selling under execution; for empanelling grand juries, advertising and attending elections, serving all public orders of all courts in the county, and for all other public services not otherwise particularly provided for, a sum not exceeding fifty dollars, to be allowed by the district court, and paid out of the county treasury.

TO CORONERS,

For taking an inquisition on a dead body, ten dollars; for all services done by them, the same fees as are allowed to sheriffs for similar services.

TO CONSTABLES,

For serving each warrant or summons, one dollar; for summoning each witness, fifty cents; for executing a mittimus in criminal cases, one dollar; for serving an attachment, one dollar and fifty cents; for taking bonds, when necessary, seventy-five cents; for levying execution, one dollar; for making money on execution, for all sums not exceeding twenty dollars, one dollar; for all sums over twenty and not exceeding one hundred dollars, five per cent; for summoning coroner's inquest, to be paid by the county, three dollars; for conveying a criminal to jail, for every mile going and returning, twelve and a half cents; for each day's attendance on courts, when summoned by the sheriff, to be paid out of the county treasury, two dollars.

TO THE CHIEF JUSTICE OF THE COUNTY COURTS,

For each suit commenced in said court, one dollar to be taxed in the bill of costs, and paid by the party cast.

SEC. 2d. The fees herein before mentioned shall be taxed and allowed in the bill of costs, in all suits or actions, where the services, respectively, shall have been rendered; but not more than one copy of any matter shall be allowed in the bill of costs, neither shall the clerk tax more than one attorney's fee in the bill of costs; and if any party, or their attorney, shall take out copies of their own declarations or pleadings, or of their own papers, in any cause, or of any common order made in such cause, the charge of such copies shall not be allowed in the bill of costs.

SEC. 3d. Every clerk and sheriff shall keep a fee book, and shall enter therein every fee for each and every distinct service; and said fee book shall be at all times open for the inspection of any person wishing to see the account of fees charged against him therein; none of the fees herein before mentioned shall be payable until there be produced, or ready to be produced, a bill in writing, containing the particulars of such fees, signed by the proper officer.

SEC. 4th. It shall be lawful for the clerks of the several courts of this republic, when suits or causes are determined, and the fees not paid by the party from whom they are due, to make out executions, directed to the sheriff or other proper officer of the county, where the party resides, and the sheriff or other proper officer shall execute and return such executions as in other cases, provided that a copy of the bill of costs is annexed to such executions.

SEC. 5th. The clerks of each and every district shall, before issuing any original process to bring any person to any suit or action, demand and receive of the plaintiff in such suit or action, a tax of three dollars on all such process; and the clerks of the county courts shall, in like manner, demand and receive one dollar, on all such process issuing out of any county court; which tax, so collected, shall be paid into the county treasury of the proper county. Any clerk who shall fail or neglect to demand and receive the tax afore-said, shall be held responsible for said tax, in the same manner as if he had actually received the same; and in every case wherein the plaintiff shall recover, the said tax shall be included in the bill of costs; and any officer herein named, who shall charge and receive a greater fee than is herein allowed, shall, upon conviction thereof, before any court of this republic, forfeit and pay a fine of one hundred dollars, and be deprived of his office.

IRA INGRAM,
Speaker of the house of representatives.

RICHARD ELLIS,
President pro tem. of the senate.

Approved Dec. 19, 1836.

SAM. HOUSTON.

AN ACT,

Organizing Justices' Courts, and defining the powers and jurisdiction of the same, and also creating and defining the office and powers of commissioners of roads and revenue.

SEC. 1. *Be it enacted by the senate and house of representatives of the republic of Texas, in congress assembled,* That there shall be elected, by the qualified electors of each militia captain's district, two justices of the peace for their respective districts, who shall be commissioned by the president, and shall hold their offices for a period of two years, and shall take the oath prescribed by law for all officers of this republic. It shall be lawful for the said justices so elected, after taking the oath of office, to enter immediately upon the discharge of their duties; and their acts shall be as valid in law, before they receive commissions from the president, as afterwards.

SEC. 2. In all cases where any person has been elected justice of the peace, and neglects to qualify himself within twenty days, after notice of such election, the election shall be deemed void, and the chief justice of the county court shall order a new election.

SEC. 3. Any justice of the peace who shall be guilty of any malconduct or misdemeanor in office, may be prosecuted by presentment of a grand jury, in the district court of the proper county, and on conviction thereof shall vacate his office, and be thereafter rendered incapable of holding the office of justice of the peace in this republic.

SEC. 4. The justices of the peace shall be conservators of the peace within their respective counties, and shall have power to take all manner of recognizance, with or without security, for good behaviour to keep the peace, or for appearance at the proper court, to answer charges exhibited, or crimes committed in the view of such justices; and in case any person shall refuse to enter into recognizance as aforesaid, and to find security when required, it shall be lawful for justices of the peace to commit the person so refusing to the county jail, there to remain until he shall comply with the order of such justice; and all recognizance so taken, shall be certified to the proper court for the county, at the next term thereafter; and if any person shall forfeit his recognizance, it shall be sent and certified with the record of default or cause of forfeiture, by the justice, to the proper court without delay.

SEC. 5. Any justice of the peace shall, by warrant under his hand, cause any person charged on oath of having committed or being suspected of any crime or misdemeanor, to be apprehended and brought before him; and if, in the opinion of such justice, there is sufficient cause to commit such person to the county jail, where such offence is not bailable, or where the offender is unable or unwilling to give bail, to appear before the proper court, to answer to the crime charged.

SEC. 6. Any justice of the peace shall issue a search warrant for stolen goods, on the oath of any credible person, particularly describing the place or persons suspected and intended to be searched, and the article for which search is made.

SEC. 7. When any person charged with a crime shall be brought before any justice, he shall take the voluntary information of the accused in writing, and the information on oath of all witnesses that appear, concerning the crime alleged to have been committed; and the accused shall have the privilege of putting any questions he thinks proper, which questions and answers shall be written down. It shall be the duty of the justice to transmit a copy of all such examinations to the next succeeding term of the proper court.

SEC. 8. If any person, charged with a criminal offence, shall remove or escape from the county where such offence is alleged to have been committed, into another county, it shall be the duty of any justice of the peace for the county where such person may be, to endorse the warrant of any justice of the peace where the offence was committed, which shall be sufficient authority for arresting such offender, in any place within the jurisdiction of such justice; and such criminal shall be carried to the county where the offence was committed, for examination. Subpoenas for witnesses may issue to any county, on the part of the republic, where it is necessary for bringing an offender to justice, which shall be executed by any officer authorized to execute process in the county where such witness resides; and any justice of the peace of the county to which any offender may have removed or escaped, shall, on the oath of any credible person, arrest and have conveyed to the proper county for examination, any person charged with crime.

SEC. 9. Justices of the peace shall have jurisdiction for all suits and actions for the recovery of money on any account, bond, bill, promissory note, or other written contract, covenant, or agreement whatsoever, or for specific articles, where the sum demanded does not exceed one hundred dollars.

SEC. 10. All suits and actions before a justice of the peace, shall be commenced and executed and returned in the same manner, and under the same penalties, as provided by the ninth section of the "act establishing the jurisdiction and powers of the district court," so far as is consistent with this act.

SEC. 11. All process from a justice of the peace, in civil suits, shall be under the hand and seal of such justice, directed to the officer whose duty it shall be to execute the same, shall be returnable at a certain time and place therein named, not less than ten, nor more than thirty days from the time of issuing the same; and on return thereof, the justice shall proceed to hear and, determine the case on its merits, if the parties appear; give judgment by default, if the defendant fail to appear and contest the plaintiff's demand, or enter judgment of "non suit" against the plaintiff if he fail to appear and prosecute his claim, and shall issue execution against the goods and chattels of the party against whom judgment is so entered, for the amount of judgment and cost, or costs alone, as the case may require, returnable at the time and place to be therein stated, not less than fifteen nor more than thirty days. Any justice may, for good cause shown, on oath or affirmation, adjourn the trial of any cause to a time not exceeding ten days.

SEC. 12. No person shall be sued before any justice of the peace, except within the district where he resides, or the district where the debt was contracted, if in the same county.

SEC. 13. On the trial of any cause before a justice of the peace, if other satisfactory evidence cannot be had concerning the matter in controversy, the justices shall proceed to examine the parties or either of them, on oath, and give such judgment as may appear to be just and equitable.

SEC. 14. Every justice of the peace shall make a fair record, in a book that he shall keep for that purpose, of the proceedings in all suits and examinations had before him.

SEC. 15. Any justice of the peace, before whom any case is pending, shall issue subpoenas for all witnesses required by either party residing within the county; and in case any witness required resides without the county, may, provided reasonable and sufficient notice has been given to the adverse party, of the time and place of taking the depositions of such witness, issue a commission to some justice of the county in which such witness resides, to take his or her deposition; which deposition, so taken and returned, shall be read in evidence; and the provisions respecting witnesses of the "act establishing the jurisdiction and powers of the district courts," shall apply in all cases before a justice of the peace, so far as they are not inconsistent with this act.

SEC. 16. Any justice of the peace may grant a stay of execution issued by himself, for all sums under twenty dollars, twenty days; and over twenty dollars and under fifty dollars, forty days; all sums over fifty dollars, sixty days; provided the defendant shall enter into bond, with security, to be approved by the justice, in the penalty of double the amount of the judgment, including interest and costs, conditioned for the payment of the same; and in case the money is not paid at the end of such stay, execution shall issue against the principal and security, for the judgment, with interest and all costs. All judgments rendered by any justice of the peace, shall bear legal interest until paid.

SEC. 17. Any party may appeal from the decision of any justice, to the next term of the county court for the county, where the sum in controversy shall exceed twenty dollars; and the case shall be tried de novo, on giving bond with security, to be approved by the justice, payable to the adverse party, conditioned for the prosecution of such appeal to effect; and the payment of such judgment, with the interest, and all costs and damages, in case the same shall be affirmed; and if the defendant be the party who appeals, and judgment be rendered for the plaintiff in the original suit, ten per cent damages upon the amount shall be included in such judgment. If the judgment of the county court be for the defendant in the original suit, he shall recover full costs.

SEC. 18. Every justice of the peace, from whose decision an appeal is taken, shall, on or before the next term of the county court, file with the clerk thereof, a certified copy of all the proceedings in such case.

SEC. 19. In cases of emergency, justices of the peace may depute any reputable person to execute any process issued by them.

SEC. 20. All fines and penalties assessed by virtue of this act, shall be paid into the county treasury of the proper county.

SEC. 21. It shall be the duty of every justice of the peace in this republic, on the first Monday of January in every year, to make a return to the county treasurer of his county, of all fines and penalties which he shall have assessed during the twelve months preceding, and to pay so much thereof as he shall have collected; and any justice who shall fail to make such return, and pay over the money by him received as aforesaid, shall be deemed guilty of a misdemeanor in office, and on conviction thereof, shall be removed in the manner prescribed in this act.

SEC. 22. When from any cause a justice of the peace shall vacate his office, all the books, records, and papers appertaining to his office, shall be transferred to the next justice of the same district, who shall complete the business of such justice, in the same manner as if originally commenced by himself.

SEC. 23. *Be it further enacted*, That in all cases where the defendant appears, he shall plead, in offset, all debts known to be due him by the plaintiff; and the justice shall render judgment for such sum as may appear to be due, either to the plaintiff or the defendant, as the evidence may require; and in case of a failure of any defendant or defendants so to plead his debt or demand, in offset, the said debt or demand shall not be recoverable thereafter: *provided*, however, that in all cases the said party may sue for and recover the same so due him, if he can show good and satisfactory cause why he did not plead such due or demand in compensation on the day of trial.

SEC. 24. No justice shall sit in judgment in any suit in which he may be interested, or where he may be related in the third degree to either plaintiff or defendant; and in all such cases the suit shall be tried by the justice of the precinct not so interested or related; and in case both of said justices shall be so interested or related, then, and in that case, the suit shall be tried and determined by the justices nearest adjoining, not so interested or related; and for the further government of the justices' court, the rules prescribed in an act establishing the jurisdiction and powers of the district courts, shall apply in all cases, when they are not inconsistent with this act.

SEC. 25. County commissioners, the justices of the peace, and the chief justice of the county court, shall constitute a board of commissioners for their respective counties; which board shall have the entire superintendence and control of roads, highways, ferries, and bridges, and of the poor within said counties.

SEC. 26. The said board of commissioners shall meet at the court house of their respective counties, in the months of January, April, July, and October, of each year, on such days as shall be designated by the president of the board; and when so assembled, shall have authority to establish ferries, determine the tolls of the same, to order the laying out of roads where necessary, direct where bridges shall be built, and contract for building the same, at the expense of the county; to discontinue all roads now or hereafter made, that are deemed useless; and to alter roads so as to make them more useful.

SEC. 27. The chief justice of the county court shall be ex-officio president of the board, and shall cause a record to be made of the proceedings of the board, which record shall be made by the clerk of the county court. In the absence of the president of the board, a president pro tempore shall be chosen.

SEC. 28. A majority of justices shall be necessary to constitute a board; and if any justice fail to attend the meetings of said board, he shall forfeit and pay a fine to the county treasury of not less than twenty-five nor more than fifty dollars, recoverable before any justice of the peace of the county, unless in the opinion of said board, he shall render a reasonable excuse.

SEC. 29. It shall be the duty of said board of commissioners to provide, at the expense of the county, for the support of indigent, lame, and blind persons, who are unable to support themselves.

SEC. 30. The said board of commissioners shall, in the month of January of each year, levy a tax, which shall be sufficient to discharge the demands on their respective counties, upon the same persons and property as are subject to a state tax, which shall be assessed and collected by the same officers and in the same manner that taxes due to the republic are collected, and shall be paid into the hands of the county treasurer at the same time, and under the same regulations and restrictions as may be provided by law for the due collection and payment of taxes levied by the republic.

IRA INGRAM,

Speaker of the house of representatives.

RICHARD ELLIS,

President pro tem. of the senate.

Approved Dec. 20, 1836.

SAM. HOUSTON.

AN ACT,

To raise a Revenue by Impost duties.

SEC. 1. *Be it enacted by the senate and house of representatives of the republic of Texas, in congress assembled,* That there shall be, and there is hereby imposed, assessed and levied, upon all articles which may be imported into this republic from and after the first day of June next, the following duties, to wit: Upon all wines and spiritous and malt liquors, an ad valorem duly upon invoice cost of forty-five per centum: upon all silk goods, and manufactures of every description

159

made of silk, an ad valorem duty of fifty per cent: upon all sugar and coffee, two and a half per cent: upon teas, twenty-five per cent, per pound: upon bread stuffs, one per cent: upon iron and castings, ten per cent: upon all-coarse clothing, coarse shirtings, coarse shoes, and brogans, blankets, kersies, satinetts, and clothes formed of a mixture of cotton and wool, ten per cent: upon all other goods, wares, and merchandise, not herein specially enumerated, an ad valorem duty of twenty per cent, upon the invoice cost.

SEC. 2. *Be it further enacted*, That there shall be assessed, levied, and collected, upon all vessels of the burthen of ten tons and upwards, arriving in any port in Texas from a foreign port, the sum of twenty-five cents per ton.

SEC. 3. *Be it further enacted*, That it shall be the duty of the president, by and with the advice and consent of the senate, to appoint for each and every district, such revenue officers as may be necessary and proper, for the collection of the revenue, each of whom shall take an oath of office before entering upon his duties, and for the punctual paying over to the proper authorities, all such money as may be by them respectively collected.

SEC. 4. *Be it further enacted*, That it shall be the duty of the several collectors, to receive the orders of the auditor upon the treasury of the republic, when offered by importers in payment of duties at the time of importation; but should the duties not be promptly paid in this manner, the collectors shall retain possession of all merchandise imported, for the space of ninety days; if, at the expiration of that time, the duties shall not be paid, they shall be sold at public auction by the collector, or so much thereof as will pay the duties thereon.

SEC. 5. *Be it further enacted*, That the secretary of the treasury shall, under the direction of the president, give the officers who may be appointed by virtue of this act, much instructions, from time to time, as may be necessary to bring this system into practical and useful effect.

IRA INGRAM,
Speaker of the house of representatives.

RICHARD ELLIS,
President pro tem. of the senate.

Approved Dec. 20, 1836.

SAM. HOUSTON.

LAWS

AN ACT,

Organizing the inferior Courts, and defining the powers and jurisdiction of the same.

SEC. 1. *Be it enacted by the senate and house of representatives of the republic of Texas, in congress assembled,* That there shall be established, in the several counties of this republic, an inferior court of law, which shall be styled the County Court of the county of ——— , to be composed of one chief justice, who shall be elected by joint ballot of both houses of congress, and shall hold his office for a period of four years, and two associate justices, who shall be selected by a majority of the justices of the peace of each county, from among their own body, at the beginning of each and every year, and the justices so selected shall attend said county courts, or pay a fine to be assessed by the chief justice not exceeding one hundred dollars.

SEC. 2. The chief justices of said courts shall be commissioned by the president and may be sworn into office by any primary judge, heretofore appointed by law or any legally authorized person.

SEC. 3. The justices of said court shall receive, for their services, the sum of three dollars for each day they are attending to hold a court according to law, to be paid from the treasury of the proper county, on the certificate of the clerk of the said court; and for all other duties, they are authorized or required to perform, they shall receive such compensation as may be provided by law.

SEC. 4. A majority of the justices of said court shall be necessary to constitute a court, and in case a sufficient number should not attend on the first day of any term, the sheriff of the county may adjourn the same from day to day, for four days, at the end of which time, if a sufficient number do not attend, he shall adjourn the court to the next term. If from any cause a county court shall not be held at any term thereof, or the business before said court should not be completed before the adjournment of said court, all business return-able to or pending in said court, shall stand continued of course until the next term.

SEC. 5. There shall be held, at the court house of each county in this republic, a county court four times in each year; the terms of said county courts shall commence and be continued as follows — For the county of Austin, on the first Monday in January, April, July, October — For the county of Brazoria, on the third Monday in

January, April, July, October — For the county of Bexar, on the first Monday in January, April, July, October — For the county of Colorado, on the second Monday in January, April, July, October — For the county of Gonzales, on the third Monday in January, April, July, October — For the county of Goliad, on the third Monday in January, April, July, October — For the county of Harrisburg, on the fourth Monday in January, April, July, October — For the county of Jasper, on the first Monday in January, April, July, October — For the county of Jefferson, on the first Monday in January, April, July, October — For the county of Jackson, on the first Monday in January, April, July, October — For the county of Liberty, on the second Monday in January, April, July, October — For the county of Mina, on the second Monday in February, May, August and November — For the county of Milam, on the third Monday in February, May, August, November — For the county of Matagorda, on the second Monday in February, May, August, November — For the county of Nacogdoches, on the second Monday in January, April, July, October — For the county of Red River, on the third Monday in January, April, July, October — For the county of Refugio, on the second Monday in January, April, July, October — For the county of Sabine, on the fourth Monday in January, April, July, October — For the county of Shelby, on the first Monday in February, May, August, November — For the county of San Augustine, on the third Monday in January, April, July, October — For the county of San Patricio, on the third Monday in January, April, July, October — For the county of Victoria, on the first Monday in January, April, July, October — For the county of Washington, on the first Monday in February, May, August, November.

SEC. 6. The several county courts of this republic shall have original jurisdiction of all suits and actions for the recovery of money, founded on any bond, bill, promissory note, or other written contract, covenant, or agreement whatsoever, or any open account, where the sum demanded shall exceed one hundred dollars, and shall have concurrent jurisdiction with the district courts, in all such suits and actions; *provided* that no suit relative to the title of land shall he tried and determined in said court, and generally to do and perform all other acts, and exercise all other powers, lawfully pertaining to a county court within this republic.

SEC. 7. All process from the county court shall be tested in the name of the clerk thereof, shall issue and be returnable in the same manner and under the same penalties as prescribed in the act establishing the jurisdiction and powers of the district courts; and all suits and actions in said county courts shall be commenced and continued in the same manner, as near as may lie, as provided in the fore mentioned act.

SEC. 8. There shall be elected, by the qualified electors of each county, on the first Monday in February next, one clerk of the county court, who shall hold his office for the period of four years, and shall be removable for neglect of duty or misdemeanor in office, in the same manner as clerks of the district courts. Before entering upon the duties of their office, they shall enter into bond with two sureties, to be approved by the courts of which they are clerks, payable to the president and his successors in office, in the penalty of five thousand dollars, conditioned for the faithful performance of the duties of their offices; and that they seasonably record all deeds and other instruments of writing required by law to be recorded in their offices; and also all judgments, decrees, and orders of said courts, and safely to keep all records, minutes, books, papers, and whatever belongs to their offices of clerk. Said bond shall be recorded in said court and deposited in the office of the clerk of the district court, and may be proceeded upon in the same manner as the bonds of clerics of the district courts.

SEC. 9. In case of a vacancy in the office of clerk of the county court, or during the unavoidable absence of such clerk, the court in term time and the chief justice thereof, in vacation, may appoint a clerk "pro tempore," who shall discharge the same duties and have the same authority as the regularly elected clerk.

SEC. 10. The several clerks of the county courts shall be, and they are hereby empowered to administer oaths, and affirmations in all cases wherein an affidavit is necessary, as the foundation of any official act to be performed by said clerk.

SEC. 11. It shall be the duty of the clerk of each county court, to make a correct list of the freeholders of their respective counties, which shall be filed in their offices: they shall enter the names on such list upon separate slips of paper, and deposit them in a box to be kept for that purpose; at every term of said court, or on failure of a term of said court, in presence of one of the justices of said court, the clerk and sheriff shall draw from said box one by one, the names of sixteen persons, to serve as jurors at the next succeeding term of said court, and the names of said persons so drawn, shall be entered upon the minutes of said court, and the said jurors shall be summoned in the same manner as the jurors for the district court, and so much of the "act establishing the jurisdiction and powers of the district courts," as relates to jurors and witnesses, shall apply to all jurors and witnesses for the county courts, so far as suited to the organization of said county courts.

SEC. 12. It shall be the duty of the clerks of the county courts to perform the duties of treasurer, and to procure, at the expense of the county, a seal, for the use of their respective courts, with the style of the court around the margin thereof, and a star of five points in the centre.

SEC. 13. Any party may appeal from any final judgment or decision of any county court, provided the amount in controversy shall exceed two hundred dollars, to the district court, for said county, in the same manner and under the same restrictions as provided in the sixteenth section of an "act establishing the jurisdiction and powers of the district court," and the forty-second section of the aforesaid act, shall apply equally to the county courts, so far as is consistent with this act.

SEC. 14. A transcript of the record in all appeals from a justice of the peace to the county courts, shall be filed in the office of the clerk of said court on or before the first day of the next succeeding term, who shall enter the same on his docket in proper order; and all such appeals shall be heard and determined by said court, "de novo," without the intervention of a jury, on all sums under twenty-one dollars, but on all sums over that amount, a jury may be had on application of either party.

SEC. 15. The records of each day's proceedings of the county court shall be read in open court, on the morning of each succeeding day, and at the close of the term shall be signed by the justices attending the same.

SEC. 16. The several county courts shall have power to punish all contempts of such courts, in the same manner as provided by law for the district courts.

SEC. 17. The justices of the county courts shall be conservators of the peace within their respective counties, and shall have power, by warrant, to cause any person or persons, charged with a criminal offence, to be arrested, and to take all manner of recognizances returnable into the court having jurisdiction of the same.

SEC. 18. The said courts shall have power to hear and determine all motions, reasonable notice being given to the adverse party, against sheriffs or other officers for money received on execution or other process from said court, which they have neglected to pay on demand, to the party entitled to the same; and all motions against attorneys and counsellors at law for neglecting or refusing to pay money received for their clients, in any case instituted in said courts, and award judgment and execution for the same.

The chief justices of the county courts shall have power to grant the same remedial process as a district judge, provided that no such writ or process shall extend to any act of a district judge, or relate to any business pending before a district court, or which may be exclusively cognizable before it.

SEC. 19. All process from any county court shall be executed and returned by the sheriff of the proper county, and the sheriff of each county shall attend on the county court of his county, and perform all the duties required of him by law, by virtue of his office; and shall cause his deputy, or summon a constable of his county to attend each term of said court, who shall attend accordingly, or pay a fine, to be assessed by the court, not exceeding twenty dollars.

SEC. 20. The several county courts of this republic shall procure, and cause to be kept in repair, within their respective counties, a good and convenient building for holding courts, and also a suitable building for a jail or county prison, to be well secured, the expense of which shall be paid by the proper county.

SEC. 21. All expenses which may he incurred for the safe keeping of criminals in the several counties of the republic, shall be paid out of the treasury of the republic, and the certificates of the proper judges shall be sufficient voucher for auditing such account.

SEC. 22. The county court of each county shall, in term time, audit and allow, on proper proof, all accounts and demands legally chargeable upon their respective counties; and all accounts and demands, so allowed, shall be recorded by the clerk of said court in a book to be kept for that purpose, and the clerk shall issue a warrant for all each accounts and demands audited, upon the county treasurer which shall be signed officially, with the seal of the court.

SEC. 23. The county courts shall make allowance of the sums of money necessary for supplying the clerks' office with stationary, books, tables, and presses, to be paid out of the county treasury.

SEC. 24. The chief justices of the county courts shall be judges of probate for their respective counties, shall take the probate of wills, grant letters of administration on the estates of persons deceased, who were inhabitants of, or resident in said county, at the time of their decease, shall appoint guardians to minors, idiots, and lunatics, and in conjunction with the associate justices, shall examine and settle the accounts of executors, administrators, and guardians; and said chief justice shall have full jurisdiction of all testamentary and other matters appertaining to a probate court, within their respective counties.

SEC. 25. The chief justice shall hold a probate court at the court house of their respective counties, on the last Monday of every month in the year, except in cases when the county courts shall be held on the last Monday in any month, and in such case the probate court shall be held on the Monday next preceding; and they may hold a special court for the transaction of any business within their jurisdiction, provided ten days' notice is given by advertisement, at three of the most public places in different parts of the county, of the time of holding said court, and of all business to be acted on at such special term.

SEC. 26. Any person may appeal from any decision or decree of any court of probate, within ten days after such decision or decree shall have been rendered, to the district court of the county, provided such appellant shall give bond with good and sufficient security, to be approved by said court of probate, conditioned that said appellant shall prosecute said appeal to effect, and perform the sentence, judgment or decree which the said district court shall make therein, in case the cause be decided against said appellant.

SEC. 27. When any appeal shall be taken on any decision or decree of a court of probate, the clerk of such court shall immediately make out a full and perfect record of all the proceedings in such case; and shall, on the application of either party give to such party an attested copy of such record, which shall be transmitted to the district court; and the said district court shall, at the next succeeding term, hear and determine such appeal, and the decision of the district court shall be certified to the court of probate, which shall carry the same into effect.

SEC. 28. The chief justice of each county shall procure, at the expense of the county, an appropriate seal for the court of probate, and the said seal shall be fixed to all papers issuing from said court.

SEC. 29. The chief justices shall receive three dollars for every day they are attending to hold a probate court according to law, to be paid on the certificate of the clerk of said court out of the county treasury; and for all other duties they are authorized or required to perform, they shall receive such compensation as may be provided by law, and the associate justices shall receive, for every day they are required to attend a probate court, the same pay as the chief justice.

SEC. 30. The clerks of the county courts shall be clerks of the courts of probate for their respective counties, and shall record all wills and testaments and other instruments of writing, required by law to be recorded in their offices, shall give certified copies of all papers in their offices to any person applying for the same, and shall receive for all duties required to be performed by them, by virtue of their offices, such fees as may be prescribed by law.

SEC. 31. All probate business heretofore pending before the primary courts, shall be transferred to, and completed in the pro-bate court, for the county established by this act; and any of the primary judges heretofore acting, who shall refuse or neglect to transmit all such business, and all records and papers appertaining thereto, shall be proceeded against in the same manner and under the same penalties as provided in the eleventh section of the act establishing the jurisdiction and powers of the district courts.

SEC. 32. It shall be the duty of the several probate courts to compel a settlement of all estates heretofore administered on, within twelve months, and may require new security to be given, if by them deemed necessary, within six months from the passage of this law.

SEC. 33. It shall be the duty of the judge of the first instance, of each and every county to deposit in the office of the clerk of the county court of his county, every matter of record, paper, document, or thing heretofore filed in the office, not by law required to be transmitted to the district court, or to justices of the peace.

NOTARIES PUBLIC.

SEC. 34. The chief justices of the several county courts, shall be, ex-officio, notaries public for their respective counties; they shall have power to administer oaths and affirmations in all matters relating to their notarial office, shall have power to receive the proof or acknowledgments of all instruments of writing relating to commerce or navigation, and also to make declarations and testify to the truth thereof, under their seal of office, concerning all matters done by them in virtue of their offices; they shall keep a register of all official acts done by virtue of their offices, and, when required, shall give a certified copy of any record of their offices or any one applying for the same; and for all acts done by them, as notary, they shall receive such fees as may be provided by law; the seal of the county court shall be the notarial seal, and shall be fixed to all instruments and attestations of the respective notaries.

RECORDERS.

SEC. 35. The clerks of the county courts shall be the recorders for their respective counties, and it shall be their duty to record all deeds, conveyances, mortgages, and other liens, and all other instruments of writing required by law to be recorded in their offices, which are presented to them, provided one of the witnesses of the number required by law shall swear to the signature of the signer, or he himself shall acknowledge the same, which shall be certified by the recorder, and form part of the record; and all deeds, conveyances, mortgages, and other liens shall be recorded in the county where the property is situated.

SEC. 36. It shall he the duty of the recorder to give attested copies whenever demanded, of all papers recorded in his office; and the recorder shall receive, for all such copies, and and other writing required of him by virtue of his office, such fees as may be provided by law.

SEC. 37. Any person who owns or claims land of any description, by deed, lien, or any other color of title, shall, within twelve months from the first day of April next, have the same proven in open court, and recorded in the office of the clerk of the county court in which said land is situated; but if a tract of land lies on the county line, the title may be recorded in the county in which part of said land lies.

SEC. 38. All titles, liens, mortgages, or other color of title, before they can be admitted upon record must be proven by at least two subscribing witnesses, if living in the county, and if not so living in the county, then the hand writing shall be proven either before some county judge, or before the clerk of the county court in whose office such record is proposed to be made; and in all cases the certificate of any county judge; that the said witness appeared before him and acknowledged his signature, or that the hand writing of the same was duly proven, shall be sufficient evidence to authorize the clerk of the county court to enter such title, lien, mortgage, or other color of title upon record; and the said clerk for recording the same, shall be entitled to charge and receive the sum of twenty cents for every hundred words.

SEC. 39. Any actual settler, who is a citizen of this republic, who may have and hold peaceable possession of any tract or parcel of land under a color of title duly proven and recorded in the proper county, for a term of five years from and after recording of said color of title or titles, his, her, or their claim shall be considered good and valid, barring the claim or claims of any and every person or persons whatsoever, minors, femme coverts, and persons non compos mentis excepted, who shall have, and be allowed two years after their maturity, marriage, or return to a sound mind, to demand and commence an action for his, her, or their claims, and no more. A peaceable possession can only be interrupted by an actual suit being instituted and prosecuted agreeably to the due forms of law, against the holder or holders thereof: *provided* that this act shall not affect the rights of any person who may have been prevented from complying with the provisions of this law, by reason of an enemy, having, had possession of the country, or for want of a proper court or officer having been established in due time: *and provided further,* that this act shall not give validity to claims unlawfully obtained from government.

SEC. 40. No deed, conveyance, lien, or other instrument of writing, shall take effect as regards the interests and rights of third parties, until the same shall have been duly proven and presented to the court, as required by this act, for the recording of land titles. And it shall be the duty of the clerk to note particularly the time when such deed, conveyance, lien, or other instrument is presented, and to record them in the order in which they are presented.

SEC. 41. The common law of England, as now practiced and understood, shall in its application to juries and to evidence, be followed and practiced by the courts of this republic, so far as the same may not be inconsistent with this act, or any other law passed by this congress.

IRA INGRAM,
Speaker of the house of representatives.
RICHARD ELLIS,
President pro tem. of the senate.
Approved Dec. 20, 1836.
SAM. HOUSTON.

AN ACT,
Supplementary to an act organizing the Inferior Courts and defining the powers and jurisdiction of the same.

Be it enacted by the senate and house of representatives of the republic of Texas, in congress assembled, That the representatives of each county of this republic, or either of them, be, and are hereby authorized and required to administer the necessary oaths of office to the different chief justices and justices of the peace for the different counties, so soon as they may have been elected, in conformity to the provisions of this act.

IRA INGRAM,
Speaker of the house of representatives.
RICHARD ELLIS,
President pro tem. of the senate.
Approved Dec. 20, 1836.
SAM. HOUSTON.

AN ACT,
Authorizing and requiring County Courts to regulate Roads, appoint Overseers, and to establish Ferries, &c.

Be it enacted by the senate and house of representatives of the republic of Texas, in congress assembled, That the county courts of the several counties of this republic, shall have full power to order the laying out public roads, when necessary, and to discontinue or alter such roads as shall at any time prove useless.

SEC. 2. *Be it further enacted*, That whenever it shall be deemed necessary to lay out any new road, the county court shall appoint at least five freeholders or householders who shall be entrusted by the court to lay out the road so ordered, to the greatest advantage of the inhabitants, and as little as may be to the prejudice of enclosures; which road shall be opened thirty feet in width.

SEC. 3. *Be it further enacted*, That all free males, Indians excepted, between the age of eighteen and forty-five years, and all male slaves over sixteen and under fifty years of age, shall be liable to work on public roads.

SEC. 4. *Be it further enacted*, That the county courts of the several counties are hereby authorized and required to lay off all public roads into precincts, and shall, at the first session of their courts in each and every year, appoint one overseer for each precinct, and shall at the same time apportion and designate the hands liable to work on public roads, and under overseers of the several precincts.

SEC. 5. *Be it further enacted*, That it shall be the duty of the clerk of the county courts, to make out and deliver, within ten days after the adjournment of the court, to the sheriff of his county, a copy of the order of court, appointing the several overseers, and the hands liable to work under them; and the sheriff shall, within twenty days after the reception of the order, deliver to, or leave the same at the common residence of the overseer, and on failure of the clerk or sheriff to deliver such order herein directed, each shall forfeit and pay for every such failure, ten dollars, which fines shall be recovered by judgment, on motion of the solicitor of the superior court of the county in which the defaulter shall reside. The said defaulter having three days notice of said motion, without the interposition of a jury, except the defaulter shall require it.

SEC. 6. *Be it further enacted*, That it shall be the duty of the clerks of the county courts, to put up in their respective court houses, a list of the names of the overseers and their respective precincts, in their county; and on neglect thereof shall forfeit and pay the sum of ten dollars, to be recovered in the manner prescribed in the fifth section of this act.

SEC. 7. *Be it further enacted*, That if any overseer so appointed shall refuse to serve without a reasonable excuse to be judged by the county court, he shall for forfeit and pay the sum of twenty-five dollars, to be recovered in the manner prescribed in the fifth section of this act.

SEC. 8. *Be it farther enacted*, That overseers of the roads shall have power to call out all persons liable to work on public roads in their precinct, at any time when it may appear necessary to repair the roads, causeways, or bridges in their precinct *provided*, nevertheless, that no person shall be compelled to work on more roads than one in any one year, nor more than ten days in the year on any road.

SEC. 9. *Be it further enacted*, That it shall be the duty of the overseer of any road to give two days previous notice by summons in person, or in writing left at their respective places of abode, to all free male persons, as well as to the owners, overseers, or employers of slaves, liable to work on roads in his precinct, to meet at such time and place as he may appoint, and to bring with them such tools to work with on the road as he shall direct; and if any free person so summoned shall fail to attend or send a substitute to work in his place, or when attending shall fail or refuse to do and perform his duty therein, shall forfeit and pay for each and every day that he shall fail or refuse to perform his duty as aforesaid, the sum of two dollars, together with costs of suit, by judgment, in the same manner as in cases of debt, before any justice of the peace of his county; and, if a slave, the sum of two dollars for each and every day he shall fail to attend, to be recovered in manner as aforesaid, from his owner, overseer, or employer: *provided* that all reasonable excuses shall be heard and allowed.

SEC. 10. *Be it further enacted*, That if any overseer of the road shall fail or neglect to prosecute any free person, or if a slave, his owner, overseer, or employer, who shall fail to attend, or neglect or refuse to perform his duty, when lawfully summoned to work on roads, without a reasonable excuse; then, and in that case, any person liable to work on the road under such overseer, may recover from such overseer the full amount that such overseer might or could recover from such defaulter or defaulters, for his or their refusal or neglect to perform their duty on the road; to be recovered in the manner prescribed by the ninth section of this act, the one-half thereof to the benefit of the prosecutor, and the other half to be applied in the manner hereinafter prescribed by the eighteenth section of this act.

SEC. 11. *Be it further enacted*, That if any person or persons whatever shall alter or change any public road, unless it be done by permission of the county court of the county in which such road so as to be altered or changed, shall, on conviction thereof, forfeit and pay the sum of ten dollars for each month the road is turned out of its old course: nor shall any person or persons erect, or cause to be erected across any public road, any bar, fence, impediment, or fall any tree or brush on the same, and shall not remove and clear away such fence, bar, impediment, tree, or brush, within twenty-four hours thereafter, he or they shall forfeit and pay the sum of two dollars for every day the impediment remains in said road, to be recovered in the manner prescribed in the fifth section of this act.

SEC. 12. *Be it further enacted*, That when to the overseer of roads it may appear expedient to make causeways on the same, said overseer shall cause them to be made at least fifteen feet wide, and the earth necessary to cover the said causeways shall be taken from both sides, so as to make a drain on each side of the causeway; he shall erect bridges across all such water courses and other places as may appear to him necessary and expedient.

SEC. 13. *Be it further enacted*, That if the overseer of any road shall fail or neglect to keep the roads, bridges, and causeways within his precinct clear, and in good order, or permit them to remain un-cleaned or out of repair for twenty days at any one time, unless hindered by high water, bad weather, or other sufficient cause, to be adjudged by the court having jurisdiction of the same, such overseer shall forfeit and pay for every such offence the sum of twenty dollars, to be recovered in the manner prescribed by the fifth section of this act: *provided*, nevertheless, that payment of this penalty shall not prevent any person or persons who may have sustained damage by the road being out of repair, from recovering the amount of such damage from such overseer.

SEC. 14. *Be it further enacted*, That at all times the county courts throughout this republic shall have power to establish ferries as are hereinafter directed. That before any person shall establish a public ferry in the republic, he shall apply to the county court of the county in which such ferry is intended to be established, and the court, for good cause being shown by the party applying, may grant a license to establish a ferry, and shall affix the rates of ferriage for crossing all persons, horses, cattle, carriages, &c., that shall pass the same, and shall moreover require from the person or persons so applying for license, to give bond with good and sufficient security, in the sum of one thousand dollars, payable to the judge of the county court of the county in which the application is made, and his successors in office, conditioned that the person or persons to whom said license may be granted, shall provide and constantly keep good and sufficient boats or other crafts; also the banks on each side of the water course, in good repair; and that said ferry shall be well attended, for travellers or other persons to carry or pass with their horses, carriages or effects over such river or water course.

SEC. 15. *Be it further enacted,* That if any person or persons shall at any time sustain damage in consequence of any ferryman or owner of ferry, not having complied with the condition of his or their bond, the person so damaged may bring an action of debt against such ferryman or owner of such ferry, on his or their bond, in the name of the judge of the county court of the proper county, and recover judgment for so much damage as he, she, or they may have sustained; and thereupon take out execution, and cause the money to be made; and when made, to apply the same to his, her, or their own use; which bond shall not be void upon the first or any other recovery, until the whole amount thereof has been recovered. Any person who shall be detained at any public ferry through the neglect of the ferryman's performing his duty, may, by warrant from a justice of the peace of the county in which said ferry is established, recover from such ferryman or owner of such ferry, the sum of ten dollars for every such default or neglect: *provided* that any such recovery shall not be a bar to any action for damages sustained by any person, by reason of the insufficiency of such ferry.

SEC. 16. *Be it further enacted,* That if any person or persons shall establish a ferry, or exact and demand ferriage contrary to the provisions of this act, he or they shall forfeit and pay the sum of five hundred dollars for every public ferry so established, to be recovered by indictment or presentment by a grand jury in the superior court of the county, in which such ferry shall be established; and any person or persons who may have any licensed ferry, who shall demand and take a greater toll than is allowed him or them by law, or by order of the county court, shall forfeit and pay the sum of five dollars for each and every such offence, to be recovered by indictment or presentment of a grand jury, as prescribed in the fifth section of this act.

SEC. 17. *Be it further enacted*, That it shall be the duty of the judges of the superior courts of this republic to give in charge to the grand juries of the different counties at the opening of each term of the said courts, this act, and the grand juries shall present the overseers of every public road, as well as the owners and keepers of public ferries, which shall not be, or may not have been kept in such order and repair as is required by this act; and every person or persons who shall have altered any public road, without having first obtained permission so to do, as directed by the 11th section of this act; and every such person or persons as shall have erected any fence, bar, or impediment, or fell trees or brush in any public road contrary to this act; and it shall be the duty of the solicitor of the superior court, upon such presentments being made by the grand jury, after giving such defaulter three days' notice to move the court for judgment in the manner prescribed by the fifth section of this act: *provided*, however, that the court shall hear the excuse of any overseer, keeper, or owner of any public ferry, who may have violated the provisions of this section of this act; and on good cause shown for the default, then, and in that case, no judgment shall be awarded.

SEC. 18. *Be it further enacted*, That it is hereby made the duty of all overseers, clerks, and other officers into whose hands may be paid any money, arising from fines, penalties, or forfeitures, under this act, and not otherwise ordered by this act, to pay the same over to the county treasurer of the county in which the same may be, within ten days after the same may come into his or their hands, and if any overseer of the road, clerk, or other officer fails or neglects to do so, he or they shall forfeit for every such failure or neglect, the sum of fifty dollars, to be recovered in the manner prescribed by the fifth section of this act.

SEC. 19. *Be it further enacted*, That it shall be the duty of the county treasurer of the several counties in this republic to receive all moneys directed to be paid them by this act, and to keep a separate and distinct account of the same, under the title of "Road Fund;" which moneys shall be under the control of the county court, and shall be appropriated by them only for the purpose of repairing the public roads, opening new roads, building and repairing bridges, causeways, &c., in the county in which the same has been recovered.

SEC. 20. *Be it further enacted*, That the county courts through whose county large creeks or water courses shall pass, over which it may be too burdensome for the overseers, with the hands apportioned to them to work on roads, to build bridges, may contract with a proper person or persons to build a toll-bridge, for which the court shall lay the toll to be levied on all persons, cattle, horses, carriages, &c., passing over the same, to be granted to the undertakers, for such a number of years as the said court may think proper, not to exceed ten years; and the builder or builders, and their successors shall keep the bridge in constant repair during the term of the contract, and in default thereof shall forfeit all right and claim to the toll of such bridges.

SEC. 21. *Be it further enacted*, That the county court before granting a license to any person to build a toll-bridge, shall take bond in the sum of one thousand dollars, with good and sufficient securities, conditioned that the undertaker or undertakers shall build and keep in constant repair, the bridges so contemplated, for the term of years agreed upon between the undertaker and undertakers and the court; and if any person or persons shall sustain damages in consequence of the owner or keeper of any toll-bridge not having complied with the conditions of his bond, the person or persons so damaged may bring an action of debt against the owner or keeper of such toll-bridge, on his or their bond, in the name of the judge of the county court and his successors in office, of the county in which such license was granted, and recover judgment for the damages so sustained, in the manner prescribed by the seventeenth section of this act.

IRA INGRAM,
Speaker of the house of representatives.

RICHARD ELLIS,
President pro tem. of the senate.

Approved Dec. 20, 1836.

SAM. HOUSTON.

CONSTITUTION

OF THE

STATE OF TEXAS

———

We, the people of the republic of Texas, acknowledging with gratitude the grace and beneficence of God, in permitting us to make a choice of our form of government, do, in accordance with the provisions of the joint resolution for annexing Texas to the United States, approved March first, one thousand eight hundred and forty-five, ordain and establish this constitution.

ARTICLE I.

SECTION 1. All political power is inherent in the people, and all free governments are founded on their authority, and instituted for their benefit; and they have at all times the unalienable right to alter, reform, or abolish their form of government, in such manner as they may think expedient.

SEC. 2. All freemen, when they form a social compact, have equal rights; and no man or set of men is entitled to exclusive, separate public emoluments or privileges, but in consideration of public services.

SEC. 3. No religious test shall ever be required as qualification to any office or public trust in this State.

SEC. 4. All men have a natural and indefeasible right to worship God according to the dictates of their own consciences; no man shall be compelled to attend, erect, or support any place of worship, or to maintain any ministry against his consent; no human authority ought, in any case whatever, to control or interfere with the rights of conscience in matters of religion; and no preference shall ever be given by law to any religious societies or mode of worship; but it shall be the duty of the legislature to pass such laws as may be necessary to protect every religious denomination in the peaceable enjoyment of their own mode of public worship.

SEC. 5. Every citizen shall be at liberty to speak, write, or publish his opinions on any subject, being responsible for the abuse of that privilege; and no law shall ever be passed curtailing the liberty of speech or of the press.

SEC. 6. In prosecutions for the publication of papers investigating the official conduct of officers, or men in a public capacity, or when the matter published is proper for public information, the truth thereof may be given in evidence; and in all indictments for libels, the jury shall have the right to determine the law and the facts, under the direction of the court, as in other cases.

SEC. 7. The people shall be secure in their persons, houses, papers, and possessions, from all unreasonable seizures or searches; and no warrant to search any place, or to seize any person or thing shall issue, without describing them as near as may be; nor without probable cause, supported by oath or affirmation.

SEC. 8. In all criminal prosecutions, the accused shall have a speedy public trial, by an impartial jury; he shall not be compelled to give evidence against himself; he shall have the right of being heard by himself or counsel, or both; shall be confronted with the witnesses against him, and shall have compulsory process for obtaining witnesses in his favor; and no person shall be holden to answer for any criminal charge, but on indictment or information, except in cases arising in the land or naval forces, or offences against the laws regulating the militia.

SEC. 9. All prisoners shall be bailable by sufficient sureties, unless for capital offences, when the proof is evident or the presumption great; but this provision shall not be so construed as to prohibit bail after indictment found, upon an examination of the evidence by a judge of the supreme or district court, upon the return of a writ of *habeas corpus*, returnable in the county where the offence is committed.

SEC. 10. The privileges of the writ of *habeas corpus* shall not be suspended, except when, in case of rebellion or invasion, the public safety may require it.

SEC. 11. Excessive bail shall not be required, nor excessive fines imposed, nor cruel or unusual punishment inflicted. All courts shall be open; and every person, for an injury done him in his lands, goods, person, or reputation, shall have remedy by due course of law.

SEC. 12. No person, for the same offence, shall be twice put in jeopardy of life or limb; nor shall a person be again put upon trial for the same offence, after a verdict of not guilty; and the right of trial by jury shall remain inviolate.

SEC. 13. Every citizen shall have the right to keep and bear arms in the lawful defence of himself or the State.

SEC. 14. No bill of attainder, ex post facto law, retroactive law, or any law impairing the obligation of contracts, shall be made; and no person's property shall be taken, or applied to public use, without adequate compensation being made, unless by the consent of such person.

SEC. 15. No person shall ever be imprisoned for debt.

SEC. 16. No citizen of this State shall be deprived of life, liberty, property, or privileges, outlawed, exiled, or in any manner disfranchised, except by due course of the law of the land.

SEC. 17. The military shall, at all times, be subordinate to the civil authority.

SEC. 18. Perpetuities and monopolies are contrary to the genius of a free government, and shall never be allowed; nor shall the law of primogeniture or entailments ever be in force in this State.

SEC. 19. The citizens shall have the right, in a peaceable manner, to assemble together for their common good; and to apply to those invested with the power of government for redress of grievances, or other purposes, by petition, address, or remonstrance.

SEC. 20. No power of suspending laws in this State shall be exercised, except by the legislature or its authority.

SEC. 21. To guard against transgressions of the high powers herein delegated, we declare that every thing in this "Bill of Rights" is excepted out of the general powers of government, and shall forever remain inviolate; and all laws contrary thereto, or to the following provisions, shall be void.

ARTICLE II.

SEC. 1. The powers of the government of the State of Texas shall be divided into three distinct departments, and each of them be confided to a separate body of magistracy, to wit: those which are legislative, to one; those which are executive, to another; and those which are judicial, to another; and no person, or collection of persons, being of one of those departments, shall exercise any power properly attached to either of the others, except in the instances herein expressly permitted.

ARTICLE III.
LEGISLATIVE DEPARTMENT

SEC. 1. Every free male person who shall have attained the age of twenty-one years, and who shall be a citizen of the United States, or who is, at the time of the adoption of this constitution by the Congress of the United States, a citizen of the republic of Texas, and shall have resided in this State one year next preceding an election, and the last six months with the district, county, city, or town in which he offers to vote (Indians not taxed, Africans, and descendants of Africans, excepted), shall be deemed a qualified elector; and should such qualified elector happen to be in any other county situated in the district in which he resides at the time of an election, he shall be permitted to vote for any district officer, provided that the qualified electors shall be permitted to vote anywhere in the State for State officers, and provided further that no soldier, seaman, or marine, in the army or navy of the United States, shall be entitled to vote at any election created by this constitution.

SEC. 2. All free male persons over the age of twenty one years, (Indians not taxed, Africans, and descendants of Africans, excepted), who shall have resided six months in Texas immediately preceding the acceptance of this constitution by the Congress of the United States, shall be deemed qualified electors.

SEC. 3. Electors in all cases shall be privileged from arrest during their attendance at elections, and in going to and returning from same, except in cases of treason, felony, or breach of the peace.

SEC. 4. The legislative powers of this State shall be vested in two distinct branches; the one to be styled the Senate, and the other the House of Representatives, and both together the legislature of the State of Texas. The style of all laws shall be, "Be it enacted by the legislature of the State of Texas."

SEC. 5. The members of the House of Representatives shall be chosen by the qualified electors, and their term of office shall be two years from the day of the general election; and the sessions of the legislature shall be biennial, at such times as shall be prescribed by law.

SEC. 6. No person shall be a representative unless he be a citizen of the United States, or at the time of the adoption of this constitution a citizen of the republic of Texas, and shall have been an inhabitant of this State two years next preceding his election, and the last year thereof a citizen of the county, city, or town for which he shall be chosen, and shall have attained the age of twenty one years at the time of his election.

SEC. 7. All elections by the people shall be held at such time and places in the several counties, cities, or towns as are not, or may hereafter be, designated by law.

SEC. 8. The senators shall be chosen by the qualified electors for the term of four years; and shall be divided by lot into two classes, as nearly equal as can be. The seats of senators of the first class shall be vacated at the expiration of the first two years; and of the second class, at the expiration of four years; so that one half thereof shall be chosen biennially thereafter.

SEC. 9. Such mode of classifying new additional senators shall be observed as will as nearly as possible preserve an equality of number in each class.

SEC. 10. When a senatorial district shall be composed of two or more counties, it shall not be separated by any county belonging to another district.

SEC. 11. No person shall be a senator unless he be a citizen of the United States, or at the time of the acceptance of this constitution by the Congress of the United States a citizen of the republic of Texas, and shall have been an inhabitant of this State three years next preceding the election; and the last year thereof a resident of the district for which he shall be chosen, and have attained the age of thirty years.

SEC. 12. The House of Representatives, when assembled, shall elect a speaker and its other officers; and the Senate shall choose a president for the time being, and its other officers. Each house shall judge the qualifications and elections of its own members; but contested elections shall be determined in such manner as shall be directed by law. Two-thirds of each house shall constitute a quorum to do business, but a smaller number may adjourn from day to day, and compel the attendance of absent members, in such manner and under such penalties as each house may provide.

SEC. 13. Each house may determine the rules of its own proceedings; punish members for disorderly conduct; and, with the consent of two-thirds, expel a member, but not a second time for the same offence.

SEC. 14. Each house shall keep a journal of its own proceedings, and publish the same; and the yeas and nays of the members of either house on any question shall, at the desire of any three members present, be entered on the journals.

SEC. 15. When vacancies happen in either house, the governor, or the person exercising the power of the governor, shall issue writs of election to fill such vacancies.

SEC. 16. Senators and representatives shall in all cases, except in treason, felony, or breach of the peace, be privileged from arrest during the session of the legislature; and, in going to and returning from the same, allowing one day for every twenty miles such member may reside from the place at which the legislature is convened.

SEC. 17. Each house may punish, by imprisonment during the session, any person, not a member, for disrespectful or disorderly conduct in its presence, or for obstructing any of its proceedings, provided such imprisonment shall not, at any one time, exceed forty-eight hours.

SEC. 18. The doors of each house shall be kept open.

SEC. 19. Neither house shall, without the consent of the other, adjourn for more than three days; nor to any other place than that in which they may be sitting, without the concurrence of both houses.

SEC. 20. Bills may originate in either house, and be amended, altered, or rejected by the other; but no bill shall have the force of a law until, on three several days, it be read in each house, and free discussion be allowed thereon, unless, in case of great emergency, four-fifths of the house in which the bill shall be pending may deem it expedient to dispense with this rule; and every bill, having passed both houses, shall be signed by the speaker and president of their respective houses.

SEC. 21. All bills for raising revenue shall originate in the House of Representatives, but the Senate may amend or reject them as other bills.

SEC. 22. After a bill or resolution has been rejected by either branch of the legislature, no bill or resolution containing the same substance shall be passed into a law during the same session.

SEC. 23. Each member of the legislature shall receive from the public treasury a compensation for his services, which may be increased or diminished by law; but no increase of compensation shall take effect during the session at which such increase shall be made.

SEC. 24. No senator or representative shall, during the term for which he may be elected, be eligible to any civil office of profit under this State which shall have been created, or the emoluments of which may have been increased, during such term; and no member of either house of the legislature shall, during the term for which he is elected, be eligible to any office or place the appointment to which may be made in whole or in part by either branch of the legislature; nor shall the members thereof be capable of voting for a member of their own body for any office whatever, except it be in such cases as are therein provided. The president for the time being of the Senate and speaker of the House of Representatives shall be elected from their respective bodies.

SEC. 25. No judge of any court of law or equity, secretary or state, attorney general, clerk of any court of record, sheriff, or collector, or any person holding a lucrative office under the United States, or this State, or any foreign government, shall be eligible to the legislature, nor shall at the same time hold or exercise any two offices, agencies, or appointments of trust or profit under this State, provided that offices of the militia to which there is attached no annual salary, or the office of justice of the peace, shall not be deemed lucrative.

SEC. 26. No person who, at any time, may have been a collector of taxes, or who may have been otherwise intrusted with public money, shall be eligible to the legislature, or to any office of profit or trust under the State government, until he shall have obtained a discharge for the amount of such collections, and for all public moneys with which he may have been intrusted.

SEC. 27. Ministers of the gospel being, by their profession, dedicated to God and the care of souls, ought not to be diverted from the great duties of their functions; therefore, no minister of the gospel, or priest of any denomination whatever, shall be eligible to the legislature.

SEC. 28. Elections for senators and representatives shall be general throughout the State, and shall be regulated by law.

SEC. 29. The legislature shall, at their first meeting, and in the years one thousand eight hundred and forty-eight and fifty, and every eight years thereafter, cause an enumeration to be made of all the free inhabitants (Indians not taxed, Africans, and descendants of Africans, excepted) of the State, designating, particularly, the number of qualified electors; and the whole number of representatives shall, at the several periods of making such enumeration, be fixed by the legislature, and apportioned among the several counties, cities or towns, according to the number of free population in each, and shall not be less than forty-five, nor more than ninety.

SEC. 30. Until the first enumeration and apportionment under this constitution, the following shall be the apportionment of representatives amongst the several counties, viz:

The county of Montgomery shall elect four representatives; the counties of Red River, Harrison, Nacogdoches, Harris, and Washington, shall elect three representatives each; the counties of Fannin, Lamar, Bowie, Shelby, San Augustine, Rusk, Houston, Sabine, Liberty, Robertson, Galveston, Brazoria, Fayette, Colorado, Austin, Gonzales, and Bexar, two representatives each; the counties of Jefferson, Jasper, Brazos, Milam, Bastrop, Travis, Matagorda, Jackson, Fort Bend, Victoria, Refugio, Goliad, and San Patricio, one representative each.

SEC. 31. The whole number of senators shall, at the next session after the several periods of making the enumeration, be fixed by the legislature, and apportioned among the several districts to be established by law, according to the number of qualified electors, and shall never be less than nineteen nor more than thirty-three.

SEC. 32. Until the first enumeration, as provided for by this constitution, the senatorial districts shall be as follows, to wit: The counties of Fannin and Lamar shall constitute the first district, and elect one senator; the counties of Red River and Bowie the second district, and elect one senator; the counties of Fannin, Lamar, Red River, and Bowie, conjointly, shall elect one senator; the county of Harrison, the third district, shall elect one senator; the counties of Nacogdoches, Rusk, and Houston, the fourth district, shall elect two senators; the counties of San Augustine and Shelby, the fifth district, shall elect one senator; the counties of Sabine and Jasper, the sixth district, shall elect one senator; the counties of Liberty and Jefferson, the seventh district, shall elect one senator; the counties of Robertson and Brazos, the eighth district, shall elect one senator; the county of Montgomery, the ninth district, shall elect one senator; the county of Harris, the tenth district, shall elect one senator; the county of Galveston, the eleventh district, shall elect one senator; the counties of Brazoria and Matagorda, the twelfth district, shall elect one senator; the counties of Austin and Fort Bend, the thirteenth district, shall elect one senator; the counties of Colorado and Fayette, the fourteenth district, shall elect one senator; the counties of Bastrop and Travis, the fifteenth district, shall elect one senator; the counties of Washington and Milam, the sixteenth district, shall elect one senator; the counties of Victoria, Gonzales, and Jackson, the seventeenth district, shall elect one senator; the county of Bexar, the eighteenth district, shall elect one senator; and the counties of Goliad, Refugio, and San Patricio, the nineteenth district, shall elect one senator.

SEC. 33. The first session of the legislature, after the adoption of this constitution by the Congress of the United States, shall be held at the city of Austin, the present seat of government, and thereafter until the year one thousand eight hundred and fifty; after which period the seat of government shall be permanently located by the people.

SEC. 34. The members of the legislature shall, at their first session, receive from the treasury of the State, as their compensation, three dollars for each day they shall be in attendance on, and three dollars for every twenty-five miles travelling to and from the place of convening, the legislature.

SEC. 35. In order to settle permanently the seat of government, an election shall be holden throughout the State, at the usual places of holding elections, on the first Monday in March, one thousand eight hundred and fifty, which shall be conducted according to law;

at which time the people shall vote for such place as they may see proper, for the seat of government. The returns of said election to be transmitted to the governor by the first Monday in June. If either place voted for shall have a majority of the whole number of votes cast, then the same shall be the permanent seat of government until the year one thousand eight hundred and seventy, unless the State shall sooner be divided. But in case neither place voted for shall have the majority of the whole number of votes given in, then the governor shall issue his proclamation for an election to be holden in the same manner, on the first Monday in October, one thousand eight hundred and fifty, between the two places having the highest number of votes at the first election. The election shall be conducted in the same manner as at the first, and the returns made to the governor; and the place having the highest number of votes shall be the seat of government for the time herein before provided.

ARTICLE IV.
JUDICIAL DEPARTMENT

SEC. 1. The judicial power of this State shall be vested in one supreme court, in district courts, and in such inferior courts as the legislature may from time to time ordain and establish; and such jurisdiction may be vested in corporation courts as may be deemed necessary, and be directed by law.

SEC. 2. The supreme court shall consist of a chief justice and two associates, any two of whom shall form a quorum.

SEC. 3. The supreme court shall have appellate jurisdiction only, which shall be coextensive with the limits of the State; but in criminal cases, and in appeals from interlocutory judgments, with such exceptions and under such regulations as the legislature shall make; and the supreme court and judges thereof shall have power to issue the writ of *habeas corpus*, and under such regulations as may be prescribed by law, may issue writs of *mandamus*, and such other writs as shall be necessary to enforce its own jurisdiction; and also compel a judge of the district court to proceed to trial and judgment in a cause; and the supreme court shall hold its sessions once every year, between the months of October and June inclusive, at not more than three places in the State.

SEC. 4. The supreme court shall appoint its own clerks, who shall hold their offices for four years, and be subject to removal by the said court for neglect of duty, misdemeanor in office, and such other causes as may be prescribed by law.

SEC. 5. The governor shall nominate, and, by and with the advice and consent of two-thirds of the Senate, shall appoint the judges of the supreme and district courts, and they shall hold their offices for six years.

SEC. 6. The State shall be divided into convenient judicial districts. For each district there shall be appointed a judge, who shall reside in the same, and hold the courts at one place in each county, and at least twice in each year, in such manner as may be prescribed by law.

SEC. 7. The judges of the supreme court shall receive a salary not less than two thousand dollars annually, and the judges of the district court a salary not less than seventeen hundred and fifty dollars annually; and the salaries of the judges shall not be increased or diminished during their continuance in office.

SEC. 8. The judges of the supreme and district courts shall be removed by the governor, on the address of two-thirds of each house of the legislature, for wilful neglect of duty, or other reasonable cause, which shall not be sufficient ground for impeachment: provided, however, that the cause or causes for which such removal shall be required shall be stated at length in such address, and entered on the journals of each house; And provided further, That the cause or causes shall be notified to the judge so intended to be removed; and he shall be admitted to a hearing in his own defence, before any vote for such address shall pass; and in all such cases the vote shall be taken by yeas and nays, and entered on the journals of each house respectively.

SEC. 9. All judges of the supreme and district courts shall, by virtue of their offices, be conservators of the peace throughout the State. The style of all writs and process shall be "the State of Texas." All prosecutions shall be carried on "in the name and by the authority of the State of Texas," and conclude "against the peace and dignity of the State."

SEC. 10. The district court shall have original jurisdiction of all criminal cases, of all suits in behalf of the State to recover penalties, forfeitures and escheats, and of all cases of divorce, and of all suits, complaints, and pleas whatever, without regard to any distinction between law and equity, when the matter in controversy shall be valued at or amount to one hundred dollars, exclusive of interest; and the said courts, or the judges thereof, shall have power to issue all writs necessary to enforce their own jurisdiction, and give them a general superintendence and control over inferior jurisdictions; and in the trial of all criminal cases, the jury trying the same shall find and assess the amount of punishment to be inflicted, or fine imposed; except in capital cases, and where the punishment or fine imposed shall be specifically imposed by law.

SEC. 11. There shall be a clerk of the district courts for each county, who shall be elected by the qualified voters for members of the legislature, and who shall hold his office for four years, subject to removal by information, or by presentment of a grand jury, and conviction by a petit jury. In case of vacancy, the judge of the district shall have the power to appoint a clerk until a regular election can be held.

SEC. 12. The governor shall nominate, and, by and with the advice and consent of two-thirds of the senate, appoint an attorney general, who shall hold his office for two years; and there shall be elected by joint vote of both houses of the legislature a district attorney for each district, who shall hold his office for two years; and the duties, salaries, and perquisites of the attorney general and district attorneys shall be prescribed by law.

SEC. 13. There shall be appointed for each county a convenient number of justices of the peace, one sheriff, one coroner, and a sufficient number of constables, who shall hold their offices for two years, to be elected by the qualified voters of the district or county as the legislature may direct. Justices of the peace, sheriffs, and coroners, shall be commissioned by the governor. The sheriff shall not be eligible more than four years in every six.

SEC. 14. No judge shall sit in any case wherein he may be interested, or where either of the parties may be connected with him by affinity or consanguinity within such degrees as may be prescribed by law, or where he shall have been of counsel in the cause. When the supreme court, or any two of its members, shall be thus disqualified to hear and determine any cause or causes in said court, or when no judgment can be rendered to any case or cases in said court, by reason of the equal division of opinion of said judges, the same shall be certified to the governor of the State, who shall immediately commission the requisite number of persons learned in the law, for the trial and determination of said case or cases. When the judge of the district court are thus disqualified, the parties may, by consent, appoint a proper person to try the said case; and the judges of the said courts may exchange districts, or hold courts for each other when they may deem it expedient, and shall do so when directed by law. The disqualifications of judges of inferior tribunals shall be remedied as may hereafter be by law prescribed.

SEC. 15. Inferior tribunals shall be established in each county for appointing guardians, granting letters testamentary and of administration; for settling the accounts of executors, administrators, and guardians, and for the transaction of business appertaining to estates; and the district courts shall have original and appellate jurisdiction and general control over the said inferior tribunals, and original jurisdiction and control over executors, administrators, guardians, and minors, under such regulations as may be prescribed by law.

SEC. 16. In the trial of all causes in equity in the district court, the plaintiff or defendant shall, upon application made in open court, have the right of trial by jury, to be governed by the rules and regulations prescribed in trials at law.

SEC. 17. Justices of the peace shall have such civil and criminal jurisdiction as shall be provided for by law.

SEC. 18. In all causes arising out of a contract, before any inferior judicial tribunal, when the amount in controversy shall exceed ten dollars, the plaintiff or defendant shall, upon application to the presiding officer, have the right of trial by jury.

SEC. 19. In all cases where justices of the peace, or other judicial officers of inferior tribunals, shall have jurisdiction in the trial of causes where the penalty for the violation of a law is fine or imprisonment, (except in cases of contempt) the accused shall have the right of trial by jury.

ARTICLE V.
EXECUTIVE DEPARTMENT

SEC. 1. The supreme executive power of this State shall be vested in a chief magistrate, who shall be styled the governor of the State of Texas.

SEC. 2. The governor shall be elected by the qualified electors of the State at the time and places of elections for members of the legislature.

SEC. 3. The returns of every election for governor, until otherwise provided by law, shall be made out, sealed up, and transmitted to the seat of government, and directed to the speaker of the House of Representatives, who shall during the first week of the session of the legislature thereafter, open and publish them in the presence of both houses of the legislature; the person having the highest number of votes, and being constitutionally eligible, shall be declared by the speaker, under the direction of the legislature, to be governor; but if two or more persons shall have the highest and an equal number of votes, one of them shall be immediately chosen governor by joint vote of both houses of the legislature. Contested elections for governor shall be determined by both houses of the legislature.

SEC. 4. The governor shall hold his office for the term of two years from the regular time of installation, and until his successor shall be duly qualified, but shall not be eligible for more than four years in any term of six years; he shall be at least thirty years of age, shall be citizen of the United States, or a citizen of the State of Texas, at the time of the adoption of this constitution, and shall have resided in the same three years immediately preceding his election.

SEC. 5. He shall, at stated times, receive a compensation for his services, which shall not be increased or diminished during the term for which he shall have been elected. The first governor shall receive an annual salary of two thousand dollars, and no more.

SEC. 6. The governor shall be commander-in-chief of the army and navy of this State, and of the militia, except when they shall be called into the services of the United States.

SEC. 7. He may require information, in writing, from the officers of the executive department on any subject relating to the duties of their respective offices.

SEC. 8. He may, by proclamation, on extraordinary occasions, convene the legislature at the seat of government, or at a different place, if that should be in the actual possession of a public enemy. In case of disagreement between the two houses with respect to adjournment, he may adjourn them to such time as he shall think proper, not beyond the day of the next regular meeting of the legislature.

SEC. 9. He shall, from time to time, give to the legislature information in writing of the state of the government, and recommend to their consideration such measures as he may deem expedient.

SEC. 10. He shall take care that the laws be faithfully executed.

SEC. 11. In all criminal cases, except in those of treason and impeachment, he shall have power, after conviction, to grant reprieves and pardons; and under such rules as the legislature may prescribe, he shall have power to remit fines and forfeitures. In cases of treason, he shall have power, by and with the advice and consent of the Senate, to grant reprieves and pardons; and he may, in the recess of the Senate, respite the sentence until the end of the next session of the legislature.

SEC. 12. There shall also be a lieutenant governor, who shall be chosen at every election for governor, by the same persons and in the same manner, continue in office for the same time, and possess the same qualifications. In voting for governor and lieutenant governor, the electors shall distinguish for whom they vote as governor, and for whom as lieutenant governor. The lieutenant governor shall, by virtue of the his office, be president of the Senate, and have, when in committee of the whole, a right to debate and vote on all questions, and when the Senate is equally divided, to giving the casting vote. In case of the death, resignation, removal from office, inability or refusal of the governor to serve, or of his impeachment or absence from the State, the lieutenant governor shall exercise the power and authority appertaining to the governor until another be chosen at the periodical election and be duly qualified, or until the governor impeached, absent, or disabled, shall be acquitted, return, or his disability be removed.

SEC. 13. Whenever the government shall be administered by the lieutenant governor, or he shall be unable to attend as president of the Senate, the Senate shall elect one of their own members as president for the time being. And if, during the vacancy of the office of governor, the lieutenant governor shall die, resign, refuse to serve, or be removed from office, or be unable to serve, or he shall be impeached, or absent from the State, the president of the Senate for the time being shall in like manner administer the government until he be superseded by a governor or lieutenant governor; the lieutenant governor shall, whilst he acts as president of the Senate, receive for his services the same compensation which shall be allowed to the speaker of the House of Representatives, and no more; and during the time he administers the government as governor, shall receive the same compensation which the governor would have received had he been employed in the duties of his office, and no more. The president for the time being of the Senate shall, during the time he administers the government, receive in like manner the same compensation which the governor would have received, had he been employed in the duties of his office. If the lieutenant governor shall be required to administer the government, and shall, whilst in such administration, die, resign, or be absent from the State during the recess of the legislature, it shall be the duty of the secretary of State to convene the Senate for the purpose of choosing a president for the time being.

SEC. 14. There shall be a seal of the State, which shall be kept by the governor, and used by him officially. The said seal shall be a star of five points, encircled by an olive and live-oak branches, and the words "the State of Texas."

SEC. 15. All commissions shall be in the name, and by the authority, of the State of Texas, be sealed with the State seal, signed by the governor, and attested by the secretary of State.

SEC. 16. There shall be a secretary of State, who shall be appointed by the governor, by and with the advice and consent of the Senate, and shall continue in office during the term of service of the governor elect. He shall keep a fair register of all official acts and proceedings of the governor, and shall, when required, lay the same, and all papers, minutes, and vouchers relative thereto, before the legislature, or either house thereof; and shall perform such other duties as may be required of him by law.

SEC. 17. Every bill which shall have passed both houses of the legislature shall be presented to the governor; if he approve, he shall sign it; but if not, he shall return it, with his objections, to the house in which it shall have originated, who shall enter the objections at large upon the journals, and proceed to reconsider it; if, after such reconsideration, two-thirds of the members present shall agree to pass the bill, it shall be sent, with the objections, to the other house, by which it shall likewise be reconsidered; if approved by two-thirds of the members present of that house, it shall become a law; but in such cases, the votes of both houses shall be determined by yeas and nays, and the names of the members voting for or against the bill shall be entered on the journals of each house respectively; if any bill shall not be returned by the governor within five days (Sundays excepted) after it shall have been presented to him, the same shall be a law, in like manner as if he had signed it. Every bill presented to the governor one day previous to the adjournment of the legislature, and not returned to the house in which it originate before its adjournment, shall become a law, and have the same force and effect as if signed by the governor.

SEC. 18. Every order, resolution, or vote, to which the concurrence of both houses of the legislature may be necessary, except on questions of adjournment, shall be presented to the governor, and, before it shall take effect, by approved by him; or, being disapproved, shall be repassed by both houses according to the rules and limitations prescribed in the case of a bill.

SEC. 19. The governor, by and with the advice and consent of two-thirds of the Senate, shall appoint a convenient number of notaries public, not exceeding six for each county, who, in addition to such duties as are prescribed by law, shall discharge such other duties as the legislature may, from time to time, prescribe.

SEC. 20. Nominations to fill all vacancies that may have occurred during the recess, shall be made to the Senate during the first ten days of its session. And should any nomination so made be rejected, the same individual shall not again be nominated during the session to fill the same office. And should the governor fail to make nominations to fill any vacancy during the session of the Senate, such vacancy shall not be filled by the governor until the next meeting of the Senate.

SEC. 21. The governor shall reside, during the session of the legislature, at the place where their sessions may be held, and at all other times wherever, in their opinion, the public good may require.

SEC. 22. No person holding the office of governor shall hold any other office or commission, civil or military.

SEC. 23. A State treasurer and comptroller of public accounts shall be biennially elected by the joint ballot of both houses of the legislature; and in case of vacancy in either of said offices during the recess of the legislature, such vacancy shall be filled by the governor, which appointment shall continue until the close of the next session of the legislature thereafter.

ARTICLE VI.
MILITIA

SEC. 1. The legislature shall provide by law for organizing and disciplining the militia of this State, in such manner as they shall deem expedient, not incompatible with the constitution and laws of the United States in relation thereto.

SEC. 2. Any person who conscientiously scruples to bear arms shall not be compelled to do so, but shall pay an equivalent for personal service.

SEC. 3. No licensed minister of the gospel shall be required to perform military duty, work on roads, or serve on juries in this State.

SEC. 4. The governor shall have power to call forth the militia to execute the laws of the State, to suppress insurrections, and to repel invasions.

ARTICLE VII.
GENERAL PROVISIONS

SEC. 1. Members of the legislature, and all officers, before they enter upon the duties of their offices, shall take the following oath or affirmation: "I, (A. B.) do solemnly swear, (or affirm) that I will faithfully and partially discharge and perform all the duties incumbent on me as _____ , according to the best of my skill and ability, agreeably to the constitution and laws of the United States, and of this State; and I do further solemnly swear (or affirm) that since the adoption of this constitution by the Congress of the United States, I, being a citizen of this State, have not fought a duel with deadly weapons within this State, nor out of it; nor have I sent or accepted a challenge to fight a duel with deadly weapons; nor have I acted as second in carrying a challenge, or aided, advised, or assisted any person thus offending—so help me God."

SEC. 2. Treason against this State shall consist only in levying war against it, or in adhering to its enemies—giving them aid and comfort; and no person shall be convicted of treason unless on the testimony of two witnesses to the same overt act, or his own confession in open court.

SEC. 3. Every person shall be disqualified from holding any office of trust or profit in this State, who shall have been convicted of having given or offered a bribe to procure his election or appointment.

SEC. 4. Laws shall be made to exclude from office, serving on juries, and from the right of suffrage, those who shall hereafter be convicted of bribery, perjury, forger, or other high crimes. The privilege of free suffrage shall be supported by laws regulating elections, and prohibiting, under adequate penalties, all undue influence thereon from power, bribery, tumult, or other improper practice.

SEC. 5. Any citizen of this State who shall, after the adoption of this constitution, fight a duel with deadly weapons, either within the State of out of it, or who shall act as second, or knowingly aid and assist in any manner those thus offending, shall be deprived of holding any office of trust or profit under this State.

SEC. 6. In all elections by the people, the vote shall be by ballot, until the legislature shall otherwise direct; and in all elections by the Senate and House of Representatives, jointly or separately, the vote shall be given *viva voce*, except in the election of their officers.

SEC. 7. The legislature shall provide by law for the compensation of all officers, servants, agents, and public contractors, not provided for by this constitution; and shall not grant extra compensation to any officer, agent, servant, or public contractor, after such public service shall have been performed, or contract entered into for performance of same; nor grant by appropriations or otherwise any amount of money out of the treasury of the State to any individual, on a claim real or pretended, where the same shall not have been provided for by preexisting law: provided that nothing in this section shall be so construed as to affect the claims of persons against the republic of Texas, heretofore existing.

SEC. 8. No money shall be drawn from the treasury but in pursuance of specific appropriations made by law; nor shall any appropriation of money be made for a longer term than two years, except for purposes of education; and no appropriation for private or individual purposes, or for purposes of internal improvement, shall be made without the concurrence of two-thirds of both houses of the legislature. A regular statement and account of the receipts and expenditures of all public money shall be published annually, in such manner as shall be prescribed by law. And in no case shall the legislature have the power to issue treasury warrants, treasury notes, or paper of any description intended to circulate as money.

SEC. 9. All civil officers shall reside within the State, and all district or county officers within their districts or counties; and shall keep their officers at such places therein as may be required by law.

SEC. 10. The duration of all offices not fixed by this constitution shall never exceed four years.

SEC. 11. Absence on the business of this State, or the United States, shall not forfeit a residence once obtained, so as to deprive any one of the right of suffrage, or of being elected or appointed to any office under the exceptions contained in this constitution.

SEC. 12. The legislature shall have power to provide for deductions from the salaries of public officers who may neglect the performance of any duty that may be assigned them by law.

SEC. 13. No member of Congress nor person holding or exercising any office of profit or trust under the United States, or either of them, or under any foreign power, shall be eligible as a member of the legislature, or hold or exercise any office of profit or trust under this State.

SEC. 14. The legislature shall provide for a change of venue in civil and criminal cases, and for the erection of a penitentiary, at as early a day as practicable.

SEC. 15. It shall be the duty of the legislature to pass such laws as may be necessary and proper to decide differences by arbitration, when the parties shall elect that method of trial.

SEC. 16. Within five years after the adoption of this constitution, the laws, civil and criminal, shall be revised, digested, arranged, and published in such manner as the legislature shall direct; and a like revision, digest, and publication shall be made every ten years thereafter.

SEC. 17. No lottery shall be authorized by this State; and the buying or selling of lottery tickets within this State is prohibited.

SEC. 18. No divorce shall be granted by the legislature.

SEC. 19. All property, both real and personal, of the wife, owned or claimed by her before marriage, and that acquired afterwards by gift, devise, or descent, shall be her separate property; and laws shall be passed more clearly defining the rights of the wife in relation as well to her separate property as that held in common with her husband. Laws shall also be passed providing for the registration of the wife's separate property.

SEC. 20. The rights of property and of action, which have been acquired under the constitution and laws of the republic of Texas, shall not be divested; nor shall any rights or actions which have been divested, barred, or declared null and void by the constitution and laws of the republic of Texas, be re-invested, revived, or re-instated by this constitution; but the same shall remain precisely in the situation which they were before the adoption of this constitution.

SEC. 21. All claims, locations, surveys, grants, and titles to land, which are declared null and void by the constitution of the republic of Texas, are and the same shall remain forever null and void.

SEC. 22. The legislature shall have power to protect by law, from forced sale, a certain portion of the property of all heads of families. The homestead of a family, not to exceed two hundred acres of land, (not included in a town or city, or any town or city lot or lots,) in value not to exceed two thousand dollars, shall not be subject to forced sale for any debts hereafter contracted; nor shall the owner, if a married man, be at liberty to alienate the same, unless by the consent of the wife, in such manner as the legislature may hereafter point out.

SEC. 23. The legislature shall provide in what cases officers shall continue to perform the duties of their offices, until their successors shall be duly qualified.

SEC. 24. Every law enacted by the legislature shall embrace but one object, and that shall be expressed in the title.

SEC. 25. No law shall be revised or amended by reference to its title; but in such case, the act revised, or section amended, shall be re-enacted and published at length.

SEC. 26. No person shall hold or exercise at the same time more than one civil office of emolument, except that of justice of the peace.

SEC. 27. Taxation shall be equal and uniform throughout the State. All property in this State shall be taxed in proportion to its value, to be ascertained as directed by law; except such property as two-thirds of both houses of the legislature may think proper to exempt from taxation. The legislature shall have power to lay an income tax, and to tax all persons pursuing any occupation, trade, or profession, provided that the term occupation shall not be construed to apply to pursuits either agricultural or mechanical.

SEC. 28. The legislature shall have power to provide by law for exempting from taxation two hundred and fifty dollars' worth of the household furniture, or other property belonging to each family in this State.

SEC. 29. The assessor and collector of taxes shall be appointed in such manner and under such regulations as the legislature may direct.

SEC. 30. No corporate body shall hereafter be created, renewed, or extended, with banking or discounting privileges.

SEC. 31. No private corporation shall be created, unless the bill creating it shall be passed by two-thirds of both houses of the legislature; and two-thirds of the legislature shall have power to revoke and repeal all private corporations, by making compensation for the franchise; and the State shall not be part owner of the stock or property belonging to any corporation.

SEC. 32. The legislature shall prohibit, by law, individuals from issuing bills, checks, promissory notes, or other paper, to circulate as money.

SEC. 33. The aggregate amount of debts hereafter contracted by the legislature shall never exceed the sum of one hundred thousand dollars, except in case of war, to repel invasions, or suppress insurrections; and in no case shall any amount be borrowed except by a vote of two-thirds of both houses of the legislature.

SEC. 34. The legislature shall, at the first session thereof, and may at any subsequent session, establish new counties for the convenience of the inhabitants of such new county or counties, provided that no new county shall be established which shall reduce the county or counties, or either of them, from which it shall be taken, to a less area than nine hundred square miles, (except the county of Bowie) unless by consent of two-thirds of the legislature; nor shall any county be laid off of less contents. Every new county, as to the right of suffrage and representation, shall be considered as part of the county or counties from which it was taken, until entitled by numbers to the right of separate representation.

SEC. 35. No soldier shall, in time of peace, be quartered in the house or within the enclosure of any individual, without the consent of the owner; nor in time of war, but in a manner prescribed by law.

SEC. 36. The salaries of the governor and judges of the supreme and district courts are hereby fixed at the minimum established in the constitution, and shall not be increased for ten years.

MODE OF AMENDING THE CONSTITUTION

SEC. 37. The legislature, whenever two-thirds of each house shall deem it necessary, may propose amendments to this constitution; which proposed amendments shall be duly published in the public prints of the State, at least three months before the next general election of representatives, for the consideration of the people; and it shall be the duty of the several returning officers, at the next election which shall be thus holden, to open a poll for, and make a return to the Secretary of State, of the names of all those voting for representatives, who have voted on such proposed amendments; and if, thereupon, it shall appear that a majority of all the citizens of this State, voting for representatives, have voted in favor of such proposed amendments, and two-thirds of each house of the next legislature shall, after such election and before another, ratify the same amendments by yeas and nays, they shall be valid to all intents and purposes as parts of this constitution: provided, that the said proposed amendments shall, at each of the said sessions, have been read on three several days in each house.

ARTICLE VIII.
SLAVES

SEC. 1. The legislature shall have no power to pass laws for the emancipation of slaves without the consent of their owners, nor without paying their owners, previous to such emancipation, a full equivalent in money for the slaves so emancipated. They shall have no power to prevent emigrants to this State from bringing with them such persons as are deemed slaves by the laws of any of the United States, so long as any person of the same age or description shall be continued in slavery by the laws of this State: provided, that such slave be the bona fide property of such emigrants: provided, also, that laws shall be passed to inhibit the introduction into this State of slaves who have committed high crimes in other States or Territories. They shall have the right to pass laws to permit the owners of slaves to emancipate them, saving the rights of creditors, and preventing them from becoming a public charge. They shall have full power to pass laws which will oblige the owners of slaves to treat them with humanity; to provide for their necessary food and clothing; to abstain from all injuries to them, extending to life or limb; and, in case of their neglect or refusal to comply with the directions of such laws, to have such slave or slaves taken from such owner and sold for the benefit of such owner or owners. They may pass laws to prevent slaves from being brought into this State as merchandise only.

SEC. 2. In the prosecution of slaves for crimes of a higher grade than petit larceny, the legislature shall have no power to deprive them of an impartial trial by a petit jury.

SEC. 3. Any person who shall maliciously dismember, or deprive a slave of life, shall suffer such punishment as would be inflicted in case the like offence had been committed upon a free white person, and on the like proof, except in case of insurrection by such slave.

ARTICLE IX.
IMPEACHMENT

SEC. 1. The power of impeachment shall be vested in the House of Representatives.

SEC. 2. Impeachments of the governor, lieutenant governor, attorney general, secretary of state, treasurer, comptroller, and of the judges of the district courts, shall be tried by the Senate.

SEC. 3. Impeachments of judges of the supreme court shall be tried by the Senate. When sitting as a court of impeachment the senators shall be upon oath or affirmation; and no person shall be convicted without the concurrence of two-thirds of the senators present.

SEC. 4. Judgment, in cases of impeachment, shall extend only to removal from office, and disqualification from holding any office of honor, trust, or profit, under this State; but the parties convicted shall, nevertheless, be subject to indictment, trial, and punishment according to law.

SEC. 5. All officers against whom articles of impeachment may be preferred, shall be suspended from the exercise of the duties of their office during the pendency of such impeachment. The appointing power may make a provisional appointment to fill the vacancy occasioned by the suspension of an officer, until the decision on the impeachment.

SEC. 6. The legislature shall provide for the trial, punishment, and removal from office, of all other officers of the State, by indictment or otherwise.

ARTICLE X.
EDUCATION

SEC. 1. A general diffusion of knowledge being essential to the preservation of the rights and liberties of the people, it shall be the duty of the legislature of this State to make suitable provision for the support and maintenance of public schools.

SEC. 2. The legislature shall, as early as practicable, establish free schools throughout the State, and shall furnish means for their support by taxation on property; and it shall be the duty of the legislature to set apart no less than one-tenth of the annual revenue of the State derivable from taxation as a perpetual fund, which fund shall be appropriated to the support of free public schools; and no law shall ever be made diverting said fund to any other use; and, until such time as the legislature shall provide for the establishment of such schools in the several districts of the State, the fund thus created shall remain as a charge against the State, passed to the credit of the free common school fund.

SEC. 3. All public lands which have been heretofore, or may hereafter be granted for public schools, to the various counties, or other political divisions in this State, shall not be alienated in fee, nor disposed of otherwise than by lease, for a term not exceeding twenty years, in such manner as the legislature may direct.

SEC. 4. The several counties in this State which have not received their quantum of lands for the purpose of education shall be entitled in the same quantity heretofore appropriated by the Congress of the republic of Texas to other counties.

ARTICLE XI.

SEC. 1. All certificates for head-right claims to lands, issued to fictitious persons, or which were forged, and all locations and surveys thereon, are, and the same were, null and void from the beginning.

SEC. 2. The District Courts shall be opened until the first day of July, one thousand eight hundred and forty-seven, for the establishment of certificates for head-rights, not recommended by the Commissioners appointed under the act, to detect fraudulent land certificates, and to provide for issuing patents to legal claimants; and the parties suing shall produce the like proof, and be subjected to the requisitions which were necessary, and were prescribed by law to sustain the original application for the said certificates, and all certificates above referred to, not established or sued upon before the period limited, shall be barred, and the said certificates, and all locations and surveys thereon, shall be for ever null and void—and all re-locations made on such surveys, shall not be disturbed until the certificates are established as above directed.

ARTICLE XII.
LAND OFFICE

SEC. 1. There shall be one general land office in the State, which shall be at the seat of government, where all titles which have heretofore emanated, or may hereafter emanate, from government, shall be registered; and the legislature may establish, from time to time, such subordinate offices as they may deem requisite.

ARTICLE XIII.
SCHEDULE

SEC. 1. That no inconvenience may arise from a change of separate national government to a State government, it is declared that all process which shall be issued in the name of the republic of Texas prior to the organization of the State government under this constitution shall be as valid as if issued in the name of the State of Texas.

SEC. 2. The validity of all bonds and recognizances, executed in conformity with the constitution and laws of the republic of Texas, shall not be impaired by the change of government, but may be sued for and recovered in the name of the governor of the State of Texas; and all criminal prosecutions or penal actions which shall have arisen prior to the organization of the State government under this constitution, in any of the courts of the republic of Texas, shall be prosecuted to judgment and execution in the name of said State. All suits at law and equity which may be depending in any of the courts of the republic of Texas prior to the organization of the State government under this constitution shall be transferred to the proper court of the State which shall have jurisdiction of the subject-matter thereof.

SEC. 3. All laws and parts of laws now in force in the Republic of Texas, which are not repugnant to the Constitution of the United States, the joint resolutions for annexing Texas to the United States, or to the provisions of this Constitution, shall continue and remain in force, as the laws of this State, until they expire by their own limitation, or shall be altered or repealed by the legislature thereof.

SEC. 4. All fines, penalties, forfeitures and escheats, which have accrued to the republic of Texas under the constitution and laws, shall accrue to the State of Texas; and the legislature shall, by law, provide a method for determining what lands may have been forfeiture or escheated.

SEC. 5. Immediately after the adjournment of this convention, the President of the republic shall issue his proclamation, directing the chief justices of the several counties of this republic, and the several chief justices of the several counties of this republic, and the several chief justices and their associates are hereby required, to cause polls to be opened in their respective counties, at the established precincts, on the second Monday of October next, for the purpose of taking the sense of the people of Texas in regard to the adoption or rejection of this constitution; and the votes of all persons entitled to voted under the existing laws, or this constitution, shall be received. Each voter shall express his opinion by declaring by a "*viva voce*" vote for "the constitution accepted," or "the constitution rejected," or some words clearly expressing the intention of the voter; and at the same time the vote shall be taken in like manner for and against annexation. The election shall be conducted in conformity with the existing laws regulating elections; and the chief justices of the several counties shall carefully and promptly make duplicate returns of said polls, one of which shall be transmitted to the Secretary of State of the republic of Texas, and the other deposited in the clerk's office of the county court.

SEC. 6. Upon the receipt of the said returns, or on the second Monday of November next, if the returns be not sooner made, it shall be the duty of the president, in presence of such officers of his cabinet as may be present, and of all persons who may choose to attend, to compare the votes given for the ratification or rejection of this constitution; and if it should appear from the returns that a majority of all the votes given is for the adoption of the constitution, then it shall be the duty of the president to make proclamation of that fact, and thenceforth this constitution shall be ordained and established as the constitution of the State, to go into operation and be of force and effect from and after the organization of the State government under this constitution; and the president of this republic is authorized and required to transmit to the President of the United States duplicate copies of this constitution, property authenticated, together with certified statements of the number of votes given for the ratification thereof, and the number for rejection; one of which copies shall be transmitted by mail, and one copy by special messenger, in sufficient time to reach the seat of government of the United States early in December next.

SEC. 7. Should this constitution be accepted by the people of Texas, it shall be the duty of the president, on or before the second Monday in November next, to issue his proclamation, directing and requiring elections to be holden in all the counties of this republic on the third Monday in December next, for the office of governor, lieutenant governor, and members of the Senate and House of Representatives of the State legislature, in accordance with the apportionment of representation directed by this constitution. The returns for members of the legislature of this State shall be made to the department of State of this republic; and those for governor and lieutenant governor shall be address to the speaker of the House of Representatives, endorsed "Election Returns of —— County, for Governor," and directed to the Department of State; and should, from any clause whatever, the chief justices of counties fail to cause to be holden any of the polls or elections provided for by this constitution, at the times and places herein directed, the people of the precincts where such failure exists are hereby authorized to choose managers, judges, and other officers, to conduct said elections.

SEC. 8. Immediately on the President of this republic receiving official information of the acceptance of this constitution by the Congress of the United States, he shall issue his proclamation convening, at an early day, the legislature of the State of Texas at the seat of government established under this constitution; and, after the said legislature shall have organized the speaker of the House of Representatives shall, in presence of both branches of the legislature, open the returns of the elections for governor and lieutenant governor, count and compare the votes, and declare the names of the persons who shall be elected to the offices of governor and lieutenant governor, who shall forthwith be installed in their respective offices; and the legislature shall proceed, as early as practicable, to elect senators to represent this State in the Senate of the United States; and also provide for the election of representatives to the Congress of the United States. The legislature shall also adopt such measures as may be required to cede to the United States, at the proper time, all public edifices, fortifications, barracks, ports, harbors, navy and navy yards, docks, magazines, arms and armaments, and all other property and means pertaining to the public defence, now belonging to the republic of Texas; and to make the necessary preparations for transferring to the said United States all customhouses and other places for the collection of impost duties and other foreign revenues.

SEC. 9. It shall be the duty of the President of Texas, immediately after the inauguration of the governor, to deliver to him all records, public money, documents, archives, and public property of every description whatsoever, under the control of the executive branch of the government; and the governor shall dispose of the same in such manner as the legislature may direct.

SEC. 10. That no inconvenience may result from the change of government, it is declared that the laws of this republic relative to the duties of officers, both civil and military, of the same, shall remain in full force; and the duties of their several offices shall be performed in conformity with the existing laws, until the organization of the government of the State under this constitution, or until the first day of the meeting of the legislature; that then, the offices of President, Vice President, of the President's cabinet, foreign ministers, charges, and agents and others repugnant to this constitution, shall be superseded by the same; and that all others shall be holden and exercised until they expire by their own limitation, or be superseded by the authority of this constitution, or laws made in pursuance thereof.

SEC. 11. In case of any disability on the part of the President of the republic of Texas to act as herein required, it shall be the duty of the Secretary of State of the republic of Texas, and in case of disability on the part of the Secretary of State, then it shall be the duty of the attorney general of the republic of Texas, to perform the duties assigned to the President.

SEC. 12. The first general election for governor, lieutenant governor, and members of the legislature, after the organization of the government, shall take place on the first Monday in November, one thousand eight hundred and forty-seven, and shall be held biennially thereafter on the first Monday in November, until otherwise provided by the legislature; and the governor and lieutenant-governor elected in December next shall hold their offices until the installation in office of the governor and lieutenant-governor to be elected in the year one thousand eight hundred and forty-seven.

SEC. 13. The ordinance passed by the convention on the fourth day of July, assenting to the overtures for the annexation of Texas to the United States, shall be attached to this constitution and form a part of the same.

Done in convention by the deputies of the people of Texas, at the city of Austin, this twenty-seventh day of August, in the year of our Lord one thousand eight hundred and forty-five.

In testimony whereof we have hereunto subscribed our names.

THO. J. RUSK, President

John D. Anderson	Edward Clark	A. W. O. Hicks
James Armstrong	A. S. Cunningham	Jos. L. Hogg
Cavitt Armstrong	Phil M. Cuny	A. C. Horton
B. C. Bagby	Nicholas H. Darnell	Volney E. Howard
R. E. B. Taylor	James Davis	Spearman Holland
R. Bache	Lemuel Dale Evans	Wm. L. Hunter
J. W. Brashear	Gustavus A. Everts	Van. R. Irion
Geo. Wm. Brown	Robert M. Forbes	Henry J. Jewett
Jas. M. Burroughs	David Gage	Oliver Jones
John Caldwell	John Hemphill	H. L. Kinney
William L. Cazneau	J. Pinckney Henderson	Henry R. Latimer

Albert H. Latimer

John M. Lewis

James Love

P. O. Lumpkin

Sam. Lusk

Abner S. Lipscomb

James S. Mayfield

A. McGowan

Archibald McNeill

J. B. Miller

Francis Moore, Jr.

J. Antonio Navarro

W. B. Ochiltree

Isaac Parker

James Power

Emery Rains

H. G. Runnels

James Scott

Geo. W. Smyth

Israel Standefer

Chas. Bellinger Stewart

E. H. Tarrant

Isaac Van Zandt

Francis M. White

George T. Wood

Wm. Cock Young

Attest:

JAMES H. RAYMOND,

Secretary of the Convention

CPSIA information can be obtained at www.ICGtesting.com
Printed in the USA
236425LV00001B/2/P